from my
Mother's Kitchen

From my
Mother's Kitchen

simple recipes for classic comfort food

contributing editor
Jenny Linford

RYLAND
PETERS
& SMALL

LONDON NEW YORK

First published in the US in 2009
by Ryland Peters & Small, Inc.
519 Broadway, 5th Floor
New York, NY 10012
www.rylandpeters.com

10 9 8 7 6 5 4 3 2 1

Library of Congress Cataloging-in-Publication
Data

Linford, Jenny.

 From my mother's kitchen : simple recipes
for classic comfort food /

contributing editor, Jenny Linford.

    p. cm.

  Includes index.

  ISBN 978-1-84597-818-1

  1. Cookery. 2. Cookery, International. I. Title.

  TX714.L5565 2009

  641.59–dc22

  2008047467

Printed and bound in China.

Designers Carl Hodson and Iona Hoyle
Editor Ann Baggaley and Helen Ridge
Production Manager Patricia Harrington
Art Director Leslie Harrington
Publishing Director Alison Starling
Indexer Hilary Bird

Notes

• All spoon measurements are level, unless
otherwise stated.

• Eggs are medium unless otherwise
specified. Uncooked or partially cooked eggs
should not be served to the very old, frail,
young children, pregnant women, or those
with compromised immune systems.

• Ovens should be preheated to the specified
temperature. Recipes in this book were tested
using a regular oven. If using a convection
oven, follow the manufacturer's instructions
for adjusting temperatures.

Contents

introduction

The foods we eat as children often become "comfort foods" later in life because they bring back happy memories of childhood and family or are associated with a particular place or time. Food is, of course, noted for its powers to evoke the past; the sensory act of tasting a dish or ingredient has the amazing ability to reconnect you very powerfully to times gone by. You might remember the favorite cake that your mother always made for your birthday or a real treat that was cooked only on special occasions for family celebrations. Often, the most vivid food memories are of simple things—the savory taste of the gravy served with a Sunday roast, the satisfying sweetness of maple syrup soaking into pancakes warm from the skillet, or the pleasurable, cool, slippery texture of a jelly eaten on a summer's day.

All around the world, the sharing of food is used to cement relationships, within both families and communities. The offering of food has been a fundamental element of human hospitality for centuries. Sitting down and eating a meal together is an important aspect of social life. Mealtimes are a simple but effective way to strengthen bonds within the family, bringing the people within a household together in a hospitable way to share food. Mealtimes offer the time and opportunity for people to talk to one another without distractions, to make those connections so important for a strong family. Sharing the table with their family offers children not simply the chance to learn polite table manners but also, at a more profound level, to learn about good social behavior and how to respect others.

We still instinctively recognize the value of food cooked in the family home. It is no coincidence that in many cultures the phrase "just like mother makes it" is the highest praise that can be bestowed upon a dish. "Home-cooking" is a phrase that carries with it connotations of simplicity, but also of comfort and a sense of belonging. Homely food—the sort of food that simply isn't offered by either fast-food joints or smart restaurants—continues to retain an enormous appeal. Today, frozen entrées offer a quick-fix solution to the question "What shall we eat tonight?" Many people, however, simply prefer to do their own cooking, taking pleasure from putting together a meal for their loved ones. This type of domestic cooking does not have to be sophisticated or complex to be enjoyed; in fact, simple, home-cooked dishes have their own, very special appeal.

In today's busy, pressurized world, where many parents juggle bringing up a family with the demands of a job, cooking can all too easily become a humdrum chore, yet another task that has to be fitted into a busy day. On the other hand, there is a great satisfaction to be had in feeding your family, cooking good, simple, tasty food, and watching it being eaten with appetite and enjoyment. Eating is, of course, essential for existence. As a parent, there is a profound satisfaction in knowing that your family are eating a healthy, balanced diet and that you are contributing to their wellbeing in the most fundamental of ways.

For hundreds of years, cookery skills were passed on from one generation to another within families, with grandmothers or mothers teaching their granddaughters or daughters how to cook. Culinary skills, such as making bread, pastry, or fresh pasta, are enjoyably learned by watching someone who knows what they're doing. Recipes, too, were traditionally often passed down. Most families have at least one inherited recipe, whether it is for something as simple as making successful mac and cheese for a weekday dinner, or a favorite, indulgent pie for a special occasion.

Cookbooks, of course, are often the starting point for many family favorites. You might be lucky enough to have a battered copy of your mother's favorite cookbook, complete with penciled notes in the margin on how the recipes worked; if so, treasure it as an heirloom, as by cooking from it you will have a wonderful window into the past. The recipes gathered together for this cookbook are all classics, chosen for their simplicity and accessibility. These recipes are not designed to "show off" your expertise, but they are all about producing delicious food simply. This collection of traditional recipes offers a chance to cook dishes that will appeal to your family and friends and form a great foundation for your own home-cooking.

Looking back to how our mothers and our mothers' mothers shopped for food and cooked, there are some simple but valuable ideas that we can benefit from following.

top ten tips from
mother's kitchen

1 *Eat together.* Eating together is a great way to cement relationships, providing an opportunity for the family to share time and conversation and laughter. This is particularly important in today's increasingly fragmented world, where things such as personal computers and electronic media offer the chance to beguile away the time on one's own. Sitting down and sharing a meal with your loved ones is a simple and pleasurable way to connect with them.

2 *Cook with children.* In the age of microwaves and frozen meals, cookery skills that were once taken for granted are being lost alarmingly quickly. Cooking with children is a great, effective way to pass on food knowledge and basic cookery skills. Of course, you don't want to make the cooking a chore. Give the child or children helping you straightforward, do-able tasks like sifting flour

into a mixing bowl, weighing out the butter for a cake, or beating egg whites until stiff, the latter task a lovely glimpse into the alchemy of cooking. Engage their senses by asking your children to sniff at the spices you need for a dish or to pick fresh herbs from the garden, so that they learn to identify herbs and spices through what they look like and by their distinctive smells.

3 *Celebrate seasonality.* Return to seasonal food shopping. Today, we live in a world where most ingredients are available all the time, albeit at a price. Fruits, such as strawberries and raspberries, that were once an annual summer treat, can now be found during the winter months, flown in from other states or even from abroad. Eating fresh fruits and vegetables when they are in season locally makes a lot of sense, as they are at their best and cheapest. A recently harvested apple, for

example, is a world away in terms of texture and flavor from an apple that's been stored for many months. By shopping seasonally you learn to appreciate the natural rhythms of the seasons and to enjoy the contrast between these different times of the year in terms of what is available. Treats such as the first asparagus or cherries of the season take on a new and special significance.

4 *Stock up the freezer.* With a little forethought and planning, it's a simple matter to cook double quantities of dishes such as stews or pasta sauces, then batch them up and freeze them for future use. These frozen dishes make a great fallback on busy days when you don't have time to cook from scratch but still want to eat homemade food. It's also very useful to have a few handy ingredients, such as ground beef or chicken breast fillets, in the freezer, in case you need to cook an extra meal and don't have time for a trip to the store.

5 *Embrace good housekeeping!* For centuries, housekeeping skills, the ability to make the most of what one had, were highly valued. Today, at least in the more affluent parts of the world, we live in wasteful times. It is well worth taking note of the more careful approach to cooking that earlier generations took. Once you've enjoyed a meal of roast chicken, for example, use the carcass of the chicken to make a flavorsome stock by simmering it in water with an onion, carrot and a few herbs. It's incredibly simple and so much tastier than bouillon cube stock, and the homemade stock can then be used as the base for risottos, soups, and numerous other dishes. Bear in mind that a little forward planning makes cooking much less stressful. Work out what you are going to cook for the next few meals and shop accordingly. One

simple way to get ahead is to make a stew or pasta sauce a day or so in advance, then chill it until required. An advantage to this is that many dishes actually improve in flavor if they are left for a while before eating.

6 *Support local food stores.* Shopping locally for your food at independent food stores is a great way of connecting to your community. If you are lucky enough to have a good butcher, fish seller, or a greengrocer near where you live or work, then it is well worth cultivating a relationship with them. A good butcher, for example, will have a range of items that supermarkets simply do not offer, such as bones for stock or cheaper cuts of meat. He will also be able to prepare meat for you, such as boning out a shoulder of lamb. You might have a favorite bakery, cheese seller, or gourmet store; if so, make sure to support them by shopping at them rather than automatically buying all your food in a supermarket. Buying good things to eat from these shops—a decent loaf of bread, a piece of artisan cheese, or some quality sliced meat or olives—makes cooking and eating at home a pleasure.

7 *Discover markets.* Going to a market once a week was a traditional way of food shopping. Hunt out your nearest traditional street market or a farmers' market, which showcases seasonal produce from local farms. The benefits of shopping at a good market is that prices are competitive and the produce noticeably fresh. Shopping at markets is a sociable occupation, which brings with it not only the fun of finding bargains but also of chatting to producers who are likely to be food enthusiasts. Ask them, or the other customers, for advice on how to deal with such things as a type of fish you've never cooked or a vegetable you have never tried.

8 *Try baking at home.* There is no doubt that baked goods taste infinitely better when they are just cooked. And that wonderful flavor, of course, is the true reward of home baking. There is nothing really very difficult or complicated about baking. Once you have mastered a few basics, such as how to use yeast or judge when you have kneaded dough long enough, then there are so many delicious things to make, both sweet and savory. It is hard to beat a crusty loaf of freshly baked bread, so good that you keep coming back for yet another slice, or scones served warm from the oven, or a crispy golden pie crust. An added extra is the wonderful smell of bread or a cake baking, a lovely, comforting aroma that entices everyone into the kitchen.

9 *Have a go at home preserving.* For centuries, people preserved food such as meat, fruit, and vegetables in order to survive harsh, cold winters, when fresh food was scarce. Today, we don't need to preserve food in the way that we used to. There is a real satisfaction to be had, however, in making the most of nature's bounty when it's plentiful. Markets or pick-your-own farms, where you harvest fruit and vegetables, are a great way of getting seasonal produce in bulk. Try making a jar of sweet, red strawberry jam or tangy marmalade to serve at breakfast or transforming vegetables into tasty pickles, relishes, and chutneys to go with cold meats. You are guaranteed a quiet glow of pride when you serve these to family or friends.

10 *Look after your pantry.* **Cooking** is much simpler and more enjoyable if your pantry is well stocked to start with. Make sure you have essential staples from which you can construct a meal. Rice, pasta, dried legumes, and canned tomatoes are all great standbys when you need to feed the family in a hurry and have only a few leftovers to work with. The same principle applies to condiments and other flavorings. Make sure you have good olive oil and vinegar, mustard, garlic, ginger, and an assortment of spices because this enables you to cook a huge range of dishes without having to track down the ingredients specially. Once you have made the initial investment, many of these ingredients will last for months and prove invaluable.

top ten tips from mother's kitchen 13

wholesome salads
& tasty sides

greek salad • salade niçoise • caesar salad • mesclun
• wilted greens • garlic mushrooms in white wine
and cream • slow-roasted tomatoes with garlic
and oregano • roast potatoes • mashed potatoes
• yorkshire puddings and horseradish sauce • roasted
mediterranean vegetables • barbecued corn with chili
lime butter

Crisp lettuce, crumbly feta cheese, fragrant herbs, vinegary olives, and salty anchovies thrown together in a bowl—Greek salad is not only healthy but also easy to make. Use unpitted Kalamata olives, if possible, as they have more flavor than other kinds.

greek salad

Put the lettuce in a large bowl. Add the cheese, olives, onions, cucumbers, and tomatoes.

To make the dressing, put the olive oil, lemon juice, salt, and pepper in a small pitcher or bowl, and beat with a fork, then pour over the salad. Alternatively, sprinkle the dressing ingredients onto the salad separately.

Top the salad with the anchovies, oregano, and mint, and serve.

note: Look out for big cans of salted anchovies in Greek markets and delicatessens—wheels of whole fish, arranged nose to tail, which need to be rinsed and filleted. If these are unavailable, use canned anchovy fillets.

1 iceberg lettuce, quartered and torn apart

about 8 oz. feta cheese, crumbled into big pieces, or cut into cubes

6 oz. Kalamata olives, about 1 cup

2 red onions, thinly sliced

2 Kirby cucumbers, halved lengthwise, then thinly sliced diagonally

4 large tomatoes, cut into chunks

8 anchovy fillets, or to taste (see note)

a few sprigs of oregano, torn

a few sprigs of mint, torn

dressing
⅓ cup extra virgin olive oil

2 tablespoons freshly squeezed lemon juice

sea salt and freshly ground black pepper

serves 4

This is one of the classic salads. There is much pontificating about the most authentic ingredients, but you can use whatever you like from the basic list. Arrange in circles on a large platter or offer single servings.

salade niçoise

Cook the baby potatoes in boiling salted water until tender, about 10 minutes. Drain and plunge them into a bowl of ice water. Let cool. Drain, then toss in a little olive oil and cut in half.

Put the eggs in a saucepan of cold water, bring to a boil, reduce the heat, and simmer for 5 minutes. Drain, then cover with cold water, and let cool. Peel and cut in half just before serving the salad.

Steam the fava beans and green beans separately until tender. Plunge into ice water, then pop each fava bean out of its gray skin. Alternatively, microwave the fava beans on HIGH for 3 minutes if fresh or 2 minutes if frozen, then refresh in ice water and peel as before. Microwave the green beans for 2 minutes, then plunge into ice water as before.

Blanch the scallions for 30 seconds in boiling water. Drain and plunge into the ice water. Alternatively, leave uncooked, but trim and halve lengthwise.

Finely slice the red onions and cucumbers. Slice the cucumbers diagonally. If peeling the bell peppers, do so using a vegetable peeler, then cut off the top and bottom, open out, seed, and cut the flesh into thick strips.

Put the lettuce leaves on a platter. Add bundles of green beans and scallions, then the potatoes, halved eggs, tomatoes, cucumber, onions, and bell peppers. Top with anchovy fillets or tuna, black olives, caperberries or capers, and basil leaves. Mix the vinaigrette ingredients in a small pitcher and serve separately.

10–12 small salad potatoes

a little extra virgin olive oil

4 small eggs

1 cup shelled fava beans or baby lima beans, fresh or frozen

4 oz. green beans, stalks trimmed

3 scallions, halved lengthwise

2 small red onions, halved lengthwise

2 Kirby cucumbers or 8 inches regular cucumber, unwaxed

2 red or yellow bell peppers, peeled (see method)

4 romaine heart leaves or other crisp lettuce leaves

about 20 cherry tomatoes, halved

1 small can anchovy fillets, drained

1 large can or jar of good-quality tuna packed in olive oil, drained

about 20 Niçoise black olives

about 20 caperberries or 3 tablespoons salt-packed capers, rinsed and drained

a large handful of fresh basil leaves

vinaigrette

⅓ cup extra virgin olive oil

1 tablespoon white wine vinegar, cider vinegar, or sherry vinegar

1 teaspoon Dijon mustard (optional)

1 garlic clove, crushed

sea salt and freshly ground black pepper

serves 8 as an appetizer, 4 as an entrée

This is probably the most famous salad in the world, with the perfect combination of salty, crispy crunch. Note that this recipe serves one person—to serve more, just multiply the ingredients according to the number of people you have at the table.

caesar salad

To cook the egg, put it in a small saucepan, cover with water, and bring to a boil. Reduce the heat and simmer for 4–5 minutes. Remove from the heat and cover with cold water to stop it cooking further. Let cool a little, then peel. Cut into quarters just before serving.

To make the croutons, tear the bread into bite-size chunks, brush with oil or butter, and rub with the garlic. Cook on a preheated stovetop grill pan until the croutons are crisply golden and barred with brown.

Put the lettuce in a large bowl and sprinkle with salt and pepper, add the lemon juice and toss with your hands. Sprinkle with olive oil and toss again to coat the leaves.

Put the croutons in a bowl and put the dressed leaves on top. Add the anchovies, egg, and Parmesan, sprinkle with pepper, and serve with lemon wedges, if using.

note: Traditionally, the dressing for caesar salad uses a raw egg yolk (see the alternative method on page 165). However, as some people are advised not to eat uncooked eggs, the recipe above has been adapted.

1 egg

6 smallest leaves of romaine lettuce

½ tablespoon freshly squeezed lemon juice, plus 1 lemon cut into wedges, to serve (optional)

2 tablespoons extra virgin olive oil

3–4 canned anchovy fillets, rinsed and drained

Parmesan cheese, at room temperature, shaved into curls with a vegetable peeler

sea salt and freshly ground black pepper

croutons

1 thick slice crusty white bread or challah bread

2 tablespoons oil and/or butter, for cooking

1 garlic clove, crushed

serves 1

Here, this salad is known as "mesclun" (from the same origin as the word "miscellaneous"). In Italian, it's *insalata di campo*—"little salad of the fields." Choose a combination of leaves—some crisp, some bitter, some peppery, some soft—and sprigs of scented herbs. The perfection of the dressing is what's important.

mesclun

Wash the leaves as necessary and dry in a salad spinner. Put in plastic bags or wrap in dry dish towels and chill for at least 30 minutes to crisp the leaves. (If washing soft leaves like arugula, do it at the last minute, otherwise they will go mushy. Most supermarkets sell them in bags, already washed and dried.)

If using garlic, put it on a board with a pinch of sea salt and crush thoroughly with the back of a heavy knife (this gives a better texture than using a garlic crusher). Transfer to a salad bowl, add the olive oil, vinegar, mustard, if using, and pepper, then beat with a fork or small whisk. Add extra salt and pepper, to taste.

When ready to serve, add the leaves and turn them gently in the dressing until lightly coated. (Use your hands, so as not to bruise the leaves and to make sure every one is well coated.) Alternatively, if you have used a large proportion of soft leaves, serve the salad undressed, with the dressing in a small pitcher. The salad can then be dressed just before eating.

note: A few tablespoons of dressing is plenty for a salad of this size—too much will spoil it. A gentle vinegar works best (especially white rice vinegar or sherry vinegar).

your choice of:

crisp leaves, such as romaine hearts

soft leaves, such as oakleaf lettuce

peppery leaves, such as watercress or nasturtium leaves or flowers

bitter leaves, such as dandelion or endive

arugula and wild arugula

soft herb sprigs, such as fennel, parsley, or basil

dressing

½ garlic clove (optional)

a pinch of sea salt flakes

6 parts extra virgin olive oil

1 part vinegar, such as cider, white rice, sherry, white wine, or red wine

1 teaspoon Dijon mustard (optional)

freshly ground black pepper

serves 4–6

An ideal—and healthy—accompaniment to most entrées, especially roast meats, this dish is especially versatile because it can be made with a variety of greens, including baby chard, spinach, mustard greens, or arugula. Simply use whatever happens to be in season. Use one of the suggested methods below, whichever suits you best.

wilted greens

method one (best for larger, robust greens, such as baby chard):

Bring a large saucepan of water to a boil. Add a pinch of salt and the greens and blanch for 2–3 minutes. Drain and refresh under cold running water. Let dry in a colander, tossing occasionally to let all the water escape (squeeze excess with your hands if necessary). To serve, sprinkle with 2–3 tablespoons olive oil, the juice of ½ lemon, and a good sprinkling of salt and pepper.

method two (best for smaller leaves, such as baby spinach, arugula, and mixed baby greens):

Crush the garlic clove, but leave whole and spear on the end of a fork. Heat about 2 tablespoons olive oil in a large pan. Add a very large handful of leaves and cook, stirring with the garlic fork, until wilted. Using tongs, transfer the greens to a large plate and continue adding handfuls until all the greens are wilted. Season with a trickle of extra oil, a squeeze of lemon juice, and a good sprinkling of salt and pepper.

1½ lbs. greens, mixed or single, such as baby chard, spinach, mustard greens, or arugula

extra virgin olive oil

1 lemon

1 garlic clove, peeled (see method two)

fine sea salt and freshly ground black pepper

serves 2–4

One of the delights of cooking with mushrooms, especially the cremino variety, is that their flavor is so good you need add very few other ingredients. That said, the perfect partners for mushrooms are garlic and cream, a truly sublime combination.

garlic mushrooms in white wine and cream

Put the oil, butter, and garlic in a large saucepan and heat until the butter melts. Stir in the mushrooms and cook for 5–10 minutes until they have softened.

Add the wine and cream and bring to a boil. Reduce the heat slightly and continue cooking until the liquid has reduced by half. Season to taste, stir in the parsley, and serve.

note: The best way to crush garlic is to add a pinch of salt, then crush it with the back of a heavy knife or a mortar and pestle. The salt draws out the juices to make a pulp.

1 tablespoon extra virgin olive oil

4 tablespoons unsalted butter

3 garlic cloves, crushed

1 lb. cremini mushrooms, thickly sliced

½ cup white wine

¼ cup heavy cream

sea salt and freshly ground black pepper

a bunch of flatleaf parsley, finely chopped

serves 4

These firm but juicy tomatoes burst with the flavor of the sun. They take no time to prepare, but need a long time in the oven and smell fantastic while cooking. Plum tomatoes have less moisture and work well, but you can use any vine-ripened variety, just as long as they have some taste!

slow-roasted tomatoes with garlic and oregano

Preheat the oven to 325°F.

Cut the tomatoes in half lengthwise (around the middle if using round tomatoes). Put them cut side up on the baking sheet.

Put the garlic, oregano, olive oil, salt, and pepper in a bowl and mix well, then spoon or brush the mixture over the cut tomatoes.

Bake in the preheated oven for 1½–2 hours, checking every now and then. The tomatoes should be slightly shrunk but still brilliantly red after cooking (if they are too dark, they will have a bitter flavor).

Serve topped with fresh basil leaves as an accompaniment to grills and fish, or use on top of bruschetta.

6–10 ripe tomatoes

2 garlic cloves, finely chopped

1 tablespoon dried oregano

½ cup extra virgin olive oil

sea salt and freshly ground black pepper

fresh basil leaves, to serve

a baking sheet covered with parchment paper

serves 4

Every good roast needs the traditional accompaniments to take it to the next level of deliciousness. Roast potatoes are always a favorite at the dinner table. This method ensures that the potatoes emerge from the oven crispy outside and light inside—just as they should be!

roast potatoes

12–16 potatoes, peeled

4 tablespoons duck or goose fat,
or extra virgin olive oil

serves 4

Preheat the oven to 350°F.

Parboil the potatoes in salted boiling water for 12 minutes, then drain and shake in the colander to roughen up the outsides.

Heat the fat or oil in a large roasting pan in the oven and, when very hot, carefully add the potatoes, turning to coat them thoroughly. Return to the oven and cook for 40 minutes. Do not disturb them before that or you will spoil their chances of crisping up. Turn them and cook for a further 20 minutes.

The secret of perfect mash is using a floury variety of potato that fluffs up properly. Older potatoes work better than new. This dish can be kept warm in the oven—250°F—for up to 2 hours if covered with buttered aluminum foil. Otherwise, cool and reheat gently, beating in extra melted butter and hot milk. If adding herbs, beat in just before serving.

mashed potatoes

1½ lbs. floury potatoes, quartered

4 tablespoons unsalted butter

⅓–½ cup milk

sea salt and freshly ground black pepper

serves 4

Put the potatoes in a saucepan of salted cold water and bring to a boil. As soon as the water boils, reduce to a simmer (it's important not to cook the potatoes too quickly), and cook for about 20 minutes. When perfectly cooked, the point of a sharp knife should glide into the center of the potatoes.

Drain in a colander, then set over the hot pan to steam and dry out. Tip the potatoes back sinto the hot pan and crush with a potato masher or pass them through a food mill or ricer into the pan. Melt the butter in the milk. Using a wooden spoon, beat the butter and milk into the mash—an electric hand-mixer sometimes helps here. Season, pile into a warm dish, and serve.

variation: scallion and horseradish mash

Beat into the mash 3 tablespoons chopped scallions sautéed in butter and 2 tablespoons creamed horseradish.

Yorkshire pudding is a British accompaniment that used to be served at the beginning of the meal to fill people up and make meat "go further." These days, it acts as a mop for gravy and pan juices from a roast. Once you've made fresh horseradish sauce, the store-bought variety will never be good enough. Grating the horseradish will make your eyes water, but the result is worth it.

yorkshire puddings and horseradish sauce

Preheat the oven to 450°F.

Put the milk, eggs, flour, and salt in a bowl and beat well.

Heat the oil or fat on top of the stove in one large pan or divide between a 6-cup muffin pan (1 tablespoon fat for each cup) or a 12-cup pan (½ teaspoon fat for each cup). Pour in the batter (take care because it will spatter). Cook in the oven until well risen (35 minutes for the large pan or 15 minutes for the individual pans). Serve as soon as possible.

To make the horseradish sauce, scrape the fresh horseradish root clean and grate it finely to give 2 tablespoons. Put in a bowl, add the vinegar and salt, and stir well. Add the cream and beat until it becomes thick and light. Rest the sauce at room temperature for at least 2 hours, but serve the same day.

1 cup plus 1 tablespoon milk

2 extra-large eggs

¾ cup all-purpose flour

½ teaspoon sea salt

4–6 tablespoons cooking oil, or fat from the roasting pan

a roasting pan, 18 x 12 inches, or a 6-cup muffin pan, or a 12-cup cupcake pan

serves 6

horseradish sauce

1 large horseradish root

1 tablespoon white wine vinegar

1 cup heavy cream

sea salt

makes about 2–2½ cups

These roasted vegetables make a tasty and colorful side dish with all the warmth of the Mediterranean sun. They are particularly delicious served with fish, but you can serve them to accompany meat dishes as well. Preparation couldn't be simpler, and the vegetables need only occasional attention while they are cooking.

roasted mediterranean vegetables

Preheat the oven to 400°F.

Put the zucchini, bell peppers, onions, and eggplant in a large roasting pan. Pour the oil over the vegetables, add a few drops of balsamic vinegar, and toss well. Roast in the preheated oven for about 35–40 minutes, carefully turning twice, adding the thyme 10 minutes before the vegetables are cooked.

The vegetables should begin to take on color and be tender but not disintegrating. Season them well with salt and pepper, and transfer to a serving dish. Add the torn basil and serve.

3 small zucchini, halved or quartered

1 medium red bell pepper, quartered and seeded

1 medium yellow bell pepper, quartered and seeded

2 medium red onions, cut into 8 wedges through the root (keep the roots intact)

1 small eggplant, cut into large cubes

⅔ cup extra virgin olive oil

a few drops balsamic vinegar

2 sprigs of thyme

fresh basil leaves, torn

sea salt and freshly ground black pepper

serves 4

Messy and delicious, barbecued corn dripping with butter is a particular
favorite with a crowd of hungry youngsters. The chili and lime add
unusual and lively flavors to this outdoor summer classic. Serve with
lots of paper napkins—this is definitely a hands-on dish.

barbecued corn with chili lime butter

Preheat an outdoor grill or a broiler.

To make the chili lime butter, put the chili sauce, lime zest, and butter in a bowl and beat well. Season with salt and pepper, then roll into a cylinder between sheets of damp waxed paper. Twist the ends firmly and chill for at least 1 hour until hard.

To barbecue or broil the corn, melt the butter in a small saucepan and beat in the chili powder and lime juice. This will be the basting sauce for the corn.

Cook the corn on the preheated grill or broiler for at least 10 minutes, basting and turning until golden brown all over, soft, and lightly blackened. Slice the chilled butter into disks and serve with the hot barbecued corn.

12 ears of corn-on-the-cob, husked

1 stick unsalted butter, melted

a large pinch of chili powder

juice of 2 unwaxed limes (use the zest for the butter, see below)

sea salt and freshly ground black pepper

chili lime butter

1 teaspoon sweet chili sauce

finely grated zest 2 unwaxed limes

1 stick unsalted butter, softened

serves 6

homely soups
& basic broths

beef stock • chicken stock • fish stock • vegetable stock
• tomato soup • cream of mushroom soup • leek and
potato soup with watercress purée • chicken noodle
soup • minestrone • scotch broth • french onion soup

A deeply flavored beef stock makes all the difference to a finished sauce. Beef blade is available on or off the bone, but for a particularly flavorsome stock, buy it on the bone.

beef stock

¼ cup extra virgin olive oil

4½ lbs. beef blade, cut into chunks

3 large onions, chopped

4 carrots, chopped

4 celery stalks, chopped

1 bouquet garni (page 41)

2 teaspoons sea salt

makes approximately 2 quarts

Heat the olive oil in a large stockpot and sauté the beef blade in several batches until brown.

Add the remaining ingredients and 4 quarts cold water and bring slowly to a boil, skimming the surface to remove the scum. Partially cover the pan and simmer gently for 3–4 hours until the stock is reduced by half and full of flavor. Season to taste.

Strain the stock through a fine strainer and let cool, then refrigerate for up to 3 days.

When you are ready to use the stock, remove the thick layer of fat from the surface.

variation: meat glaze

Return the strained stock to a clean pan and simmer until reduced to approximately 1¼ cups. Let cool. Refrigerate for up to 1 month.

Delicate soups and savory sauces benefit from a good, homemade chicken stock base. Refrigerating the cold stock overnight allows the fat to solidify on the surface, making it much easier to remove.

chicken stock

To make the bouquet garni, remove the outer layer of leek (reserving the rest for the stock) and open out flat. Put the celery, garlic, bay leaves, parsley, thyme, and peppercorns on top of the leek skin, then roll up tightly. Tie up with kitchen twine.

Put the chicken in a large stockpot with all the remaining ingredients and cover with cold water (about 2 quarts).

Bring slowly to a boil, skimming the surface to remove the scum. Partially cover the pan and simmer gently for 3 hours.

Strain the stock through a fine strainer and let cool, then refrigerate overnight.

Remove the thick layer of fat from the surface. Refrigerate for up to 3 days.

note: If preferred, you can wrap the bouquet garni in cheesecloth instead of leek skin.

a 5-lb. chicken, washed

2 onions, chopped

2 carrots, chopped

2 celery stalks, chopped

2 leeks, chopped

2 garlic cloves, peeled

1 bouquet garni (see below)

2 teaspoons sea salt

makes approximately 2 quarts

bouquet garni

a 3-inch length of leek (see note)

a 3-inch length of celery stalk

1 garlic clove, peeled

2 fresh bay leaves (or 1 dried)

2 fresh flatleaf parsley sprigs

2 fresh thyme sprigs

6 black peppercorns

These two stocks will keep well in the refrigerator for a few days and are economical to make. Most fish sellers will happily give you their fish trimmings and you can use up the leftovers in your vegetable basket.

fish stock

Wash the fish trimmings and put in a large saucepan with all the remaining ingredients and 7 cups cold water. Bring to a boil, skimming the surface to remove the scum. Partially cover the pan and simmer gently for 30 minutes (no longer, or you will get a bitter flavor).

Strain the stock through a fine strainer into a clean pan and return to a boil. Simmer, uncovered, for 15 minutes, or until the liquid is reduced by half. You should be left with approximately 6 cups fish stock. Let cool and refrigerate for up to 3 days.

2¼ lbs. fish trimmings

a 750-ml bottle dry white wine

1 tablespoon white wine vinegar

2 large carrots, chopped

1 onion, chopped

2 celery stalks, chopped

1 leek, chopped

2 garlic cloves, peeled

1 bouquet garni (page 41)

1 teaspoon sea salt

makes approximately 6 cups

vegetable stock

Heat the olive oil in a large saucepan and sauté the garlic, onion, and leek for 10 minutes. Add the carrots, potatoes, and celery and sauté for a further 10 minutes, or until softened but not colored.

Add the wine and boil rapidly for 2–3 minutes, or until the liquid is almost completely reduced. Add the remaining ingredients and 2 quarts cold water and bring to a boil. Cover and simmer for 1 hour.

Strain the stock through a fine strainer and let cool completely. Refrigerate for up to 3 days.

2 tablespoons extra virgin olive oil

2 garlic cloves, peeled

1 onion, roughly chopped

1 large leek, chopped

2 carrots, chopped

2 potatoes, diced

2 celery stalks, chopped

⅔ cup dry white wine

1 ripe tomato, chopped

1¼ cups mushrooms, chopped

⅓ cup red lentils

1 bouquet garni (page 41)

2 teaspoons sea salt

makes approximately 2 quarts

The ultimate home comfort, tomato soup needs to be made with really ripe, flavorful tomatoes—the best you can find. The citrus tang of the lemon will cut through the smoothness of the soup. Add some pesto and extra basil leaves to serve, for an Italian twist.

tomato soup

To peel the tomatoes, cut a cross in the base of each and dunk into a saucepan of boiling water. Remove after 10 seconds and put in a strainer set over a large saucepan. Slip off and discard the skins and cut the tomatoes in half around their "equators." Using a teaspoon, scoop out the seeds into the strainer, then press the pulp and juice through the strainer and transfer to a blender. Discard the seeds. Chop the tomato halves and add to the blender.

Purée the tomatoes, adding a little of the stock to help the process—you may have to work in batches. Add the remaining stock, season to taste with salt and pepper, and transfer to the saucepan. Heat well without boiling. Serve in heated soup plates and top each serving with 1 teaspoon lemon juice, 1 tablespoon pesto (if using), chives or basil, lemon zest, and pepper.

2 lbs. very ripe red tomatoes

2 cups chicken stock (page 41), or to taste

sea salt and coarsely crushed black pepper

to serve

shredded zest and freshly squeezed juice of 1 unwaxed lemon

4 tablespoons pesto (optional) (page 164)

chives, snipped with kitchen shears, or torn basil

serves 4

You could make this soup with any cultivated mushrooms, but the dried porcini and large portobello mushrooms used here give a wonderful flavor and particularly rich color. Most supermarkets stock a variety of fresh and dried mushrooms, so you can choose what you like.

cream of mushroom soup

Put the dried porcini in a bowl, add 1 cup boiling water, and let soak for at least 15 minutes. Heat the oil in a skillet, add the fresh mushrooms, and sauté until colored but still firm. Reserve a few slices for serving.

Add the onion to the skillet and sauté until softened, then add the garlic, nutmeg, and parsley. Rinse any grit out of the porcini and strain their soaking liquid several times through cheesecloth or a tea strainer. Add the liquid and the porcini to the pan. Bring to a boil, then transfer to a food processor. Add 2 ladles of the boiling stock, then pulse until the mixture is creamy but still chunky.

Heat the butter in a saucepan until melted, stir in the flour, and cook gently, stirring constantly, until the mixture is very dark brown (take care or it will burn). Add the remaining stock, 1 ladle at a time, stirring well after each addition. Add the mushroom mixture, bring to a boil, then simmer for 20 minutes. Season with salt and pepper to taste. Serve in heated soup bowls topped with a few reserved mushrooms, parsley, and sour cream.

note: If you use a blender to make soup, the purée will be very smooth. If you use a food processor, it will be less smooth, and if you use the pulse button, you can make the mixture quite chunky, which suits mushrooms.

1 oz. dried porcini mushrooms

¼ cup extra virgin olive oil

6 large portobello mushrooms, wiped, trimmed, and sliced

1 onion, halved and thinly sliced

3 garlic cloves, crushed

pinch of freshly grated nutmeg

leaves from a large bunch of fresh parsley, finely chopped in a food processor

5 cups boiling chicken stock (page 41) or vegetable stock (page 43)

4 tablespoons butter

¼ cup all-purpose flour

sea salt and freshly ground black pepper

to serve

4–6 tablespoons coarsely chopped fresh parsley

4–6 tablespoons sour cream or crème fraîche

serves 4–6

This is a gorgeously smooth and velvety soup that will suit all tastes and any family occasion, from picnics to dinner parties. To ensure a really smooth texture, it is very important to blend, then strain the soup before serving. It is equally delicious served either hot or chilled.

leek and potato soup with watercress purée

To make the watercress purée, put the watercress leaves in a blender with the olive oil. Blend until smooth. Pour into a screwtop jar and set aside until needed.

To make the soup, melt the butter in a large saucepan and add the onions and leeks. Stir well, add 3 tablespoons water, cover tightly, and cook over gentle heat for 10 minutes, or until soft and golden, but not at all brown.

Stir in the potatoes and chicken stock. Bring to a boil, reduce the heat, cover, and simmer for 20 minutes, or until the potatoes are tender. Stir in the milk, then purée in a blender or with an immersion hand blender. Press the purée through a strainer, then return it to the pan. Stir in the sour cream and season. Let cool and chill (if serving chilled, add extra seasoning) or serve hot in warm soup bowls with a swirl of watercress purée and dollop of chilled sour cream.

5½ tablespoons unsalted butter

2 medium onions, finely chopped

1 lb. leeks (white part only), finely chopped

1 medium potato, chopped

5½ cups chicken stock (page 41)

1¼ cups milk

⅔ cup sour cream or crème fraîche, plus extra to serve

sea salt and freshly ground white pepper

watercress purée

1 cup watercress, stalks removed

⅓ cup extra virgin olive oil

serves 6

The trick to producing an extra rich stock for this soup is to brown the chicken first and cover while simmering. The result is a deep, flavorsome base that suits any additions. Fine egg noodles are classic for this comforting soup, but you can try rice or matzo balls.

chicken noodle soup

Heat 1 tablespoon of the olive oil in a large, heavy stockpot. Season the chicken pieces and brown them in the stockpot in batches. Put all the chicken pieces back in the pot with the onion, carrot, garlic, and celery, and cook over low heat for 15 minutes. Pour in 6 cups water, add the bouquet garni, and simmer, covered, for 1 hour over medium/low heat. Remove any foamy scum from the surface during cooking.

Pour the finished stock through a fine strainer into a bowl and skim off any excess fat. Reserve the chicken and let cool before removing the meat from the bones and roughly chopping it.

To finish, heat the remaining olive oil in a saucepan. Add the onion, carrots, and celery, and season. Sauté for 5 minutes, then pour in the stock. Bring to a boil and add the noodles. Cook until the noodles are al dente, then add the chopped chicken. Sprinkle in the chopped parsley, stir, and serve.

2 tablespoons olive oil

3 lbs. chicken drumsticks and thighs

1 medium onion, chopped

1 carrot, peeled and chopped

1 garlic clove, sliced

2 celery stalks, chopped

1 bouquet garni (page 41)

to finish

1 medium onion, chopped

2 large carrots, peeled and sliced
½ inch thick

2 celery stalks, sliced 1 inch thick

3 oz. fine egg noodles, broken
into pieces

¼ cup fresh flatleaf parsley,
finely chopped

sea salt and freshly ground black pepper

serves 4

No one understands family cooking better than the Italians. This gorgeous soup is one of their classics—and it's a meal in itself. There are many versions of minestrone, according to which region of Italy a recipe comes from, but they are all good. This particular recipe uses pancetta or bacon for a bit of extra flavor.

minestrone

Soak the beans overnight in at least 5 cups cold water to cover.

Drain, then put in a saucepan, cover with cold water, and bring to a boil. Reduce the heat and simmer until almost tender (they will be cooked again, so don't let them get too soft). Do not add salt during this precooking, or you will have cannellini bullets. Drain and set aside.

Put the pancetta, garlic, and parsley in a stockpot, heat gently, and sauté until the fat runs. Add the olive oil, heat briefly, then add the onion and cook gently until softened but not brown.

Add the potatoes, carrots, celery, tomatoes, salt, and pepper. Add 3 quarts water and heat until simmering. Cook over low heat for about 20 minutes. Add the rice and simmer for 10 minutes. Add the cabbage and reserved beans, bring to a boil, and cook for 5 minutes, then add the peas and zucchini and cook for another 2–3 minutes until all the vegetables are tender. Remove and discard the parsley stalks, add salt and pepper to taste, then serve sprinkled with torn basil. Crusty Italian bread and a dish of freshly grated Parmesan are the perfect accompaniments.

note: Use canned or bottled beans if you prefer, but remember that they often have sugar and salt added, so keep that in mind when seasoning. They are already quite soft, so add them at the end and cook only until heated through.

1¼ cups dried cannellini beans

8 oz. pancetta or bacon, cut into cubes or strips

2 garlic cloves, crushed

2 large stalks of parsley, lightly crushed

1 tablespoon extra virgin olive oil

1 large onion, chopped

2 large potatoes, diced and rinsed

3 carrots, diced

2 celery stalks, sliced

3 tomatoes, halved, seeded, and chopped

1 cup Italian risotto rice

1 small round cabbage, quartered, cored, and sliced

2 cups shelled peas, fresh or frozen

3 small zucchini, halved lengthwise, halved again into quarters, then thickly sliced

sea salt and freshly ground black pepper

to serve

a handful of basil, torn

crusty bread

freshly grated Parmesan cheese

serves 6–8

From the land that brings us haggis, kippers, neeps, and tatties comes its famous broth. Barley is traditionally used, but here it is substituted with brown rice. Although soy sauce is never used in traditional Scottish fare, it works well with the other flavors in this recipe. You could add some herbs as well, if you like. Thyme, in particular, is good with lamb.

scotch broth

Heat the oil in a large saucepan. Add the carrot, leek, celery stalks, and leaves and cook over high heat for 5 minutes, stirring often. Add the lamb, stock, soy sauce, rice, and 1 quart of water and bring to a boil.

Reduce the heat to low, cover with a tight-fitting lid, and let the soup simmer for 1 hour. Season to taste with salt and pepper and serve with soft, buttered rolls on the side.

2 tablespoons light olive oil

1 carrot, diced

1 leek, diced

2 celery stalks, diced and leaves chopped

1 lb. stewing lamb, well trimmed of fat and cubed

2 cups chicken stock (page 41)

1 tablespoon light soy sauce

½ cup brown rice

sea salt and freshly ground black pepper

serves 4

This is associated with the French tradition of serving onion soup at wedding parties in the early hours of the morning, as a restorative after a long night of celebrating. Here is a simplified version of the recipe, the sort of thing that's ideal when it's chilly outside, people are hungry inside, and there's not much more than a few onions lurking about.

french onion soup

Put the butter and oil in a large saucepan and melt over medium heat. Add the onions and cook over low heat until soft, 15–20 minutes.

Add the garlic and flour and cook, stirring, for about 1 minute. Add the stock, wine, bay leaf, and thyme. Season with salt and pepper and bring to a boil. Boil for 1 minute, then lower the heat and simmer very gently for 20 minutes. Taste and adjust the seasoning. At this point, the soup will be cooked, but standing time will improve the flavor—at least 30 minutes.

Before serving, preheat the broiler. Put the baguette slices on a baking sheet and brown under the broiler until lightly toasted. Set aside.

To serve, ladle the soup into ovenproof bowls and top with a few toasted baguette rounds. Sprinkle the grated cheese over the top and cook under the broiler until brown and bubbling. Serve immediately.

3 tablespoons unsalted butter

1 tablespoon extra virgin olive oil

3 large onions, about 3 lbs., thinly sliced

2 garlic cloves, crushed

1 tablespoon all-purpose flour

1 quart beef stock (page 40) or chicken stock (page 41)

2¾ cups dry white wine

1 fresh bay leaf

2 sprigs of thyme

coarse sea salt and freshly ground black pepper

to serve

1 baguette, or other white bread, sliced

1½ cups freshly grated Gruyère cheese, about 5 oz.

a baking sheet

serves 4–6

hot from the stove

Think of chilly, dark evenings and this is exactly the sort of warming food you'd want to eat. The feather-light dumplings nestling in the rich, savory casserole will have everyone demanding more. A staple of British home cooking—with a touch of tangy Cheddar cheese in the dumplings to add an extra bite to the flavors.

beef and carrot casserole with cheesy dumplings

Heat the olive oil in a large casserole, add the garlic, onion, and celery, and sauté for 4 minutes. Transfer to a plate. Put the beef in the casserole, increase the heat, and sauté for 5 minutes, stirring frequently. When the beef is cooked, return the onion mixture to the casserole. Add the stock, red wine, seasoning, and bay leaves, bring to a boil, then reduce the heat to a gentle simmer. Cover and cook for 1½ hours.

To make the dumplings, place the flour and baking powder in a bowl and rub in the shortening until it resembles bread crumbs. Add the cheese, mixing it in with a knife. Add ¼–⅓ cup water and use your hands to bring the mixture together and form a dough. Divide into 8 equal pieces and roll into balls.

Remove the casserole from the heat for about 5 minutes, then sift in the flour and stir to thicken the gravy. Return to the heat, add the carrots, and stir until the casserole comes to a simmer. Place the dumplings on top, cover, and cook for a further 20 minutes.

1 tablespoon extra virgin olive oil

2 garlic cloves, crushed

1 onion, diced

2 celery stalks, diced

2 lbs. chuck steak, cut into cubes

1⅔ cups beef stock (page 40)

¾ cup red wine

2 bay leaves

2 tablespoons all-purpose flour

4 carrots, cut into small chunks

sea salt and freshly ground black pepper

cheesy dumplings

1½ cups all-purpose flour

1 teaspoon baking powder

⅓ cup shortening

½ cup sharp Cheddar cheese, grated

serves 4–6

Manhattan clam chowder is the tomato-based cousin of the creamy New England variety. Always buy your clams from a good fish seller and check them to make sure they are in the best condition. Clams should have a fresh smell and their shells should look clean and unbroken.

manhattan clam chowder

Place the clams in a clean kitchen sink filled with very cold water and the salt. Leave for 30 minutes to draw out any impurities. Drain the clams and put them in a large, lidded pot. Add just enough water to cover by 2 inches. Cover with the lid and bring to a boil over high heat. Turn the heat down to low and cook for 1 minute. Remove the lid and, using a slotted spoon, set aside all the clams that have opened. Try reheating the ones that didn't open and discard any that still don't. Reserve the liquid and pass through a fine strainer. Leave the clams to cool slightly, then remove from their shells, roughly chop, and set aside. Alternatively, you can leave the clams in their shells.

In a large saucepan, pan-fry the bacon until crisp. Pour off most of the fat, leaving 2 tablespoons. Add the onion, celery, garlic, and carrot. Season and cook for 10 minutes. Add the potatoes, tomatoes, bay leaves, reserved clam liquid, and clam juice. Bring to a boil and cook for a further 10 minutes. Add the clams and parsley and taste for additional seasoning. Serve with chunks of crusty bread.

40 small clams

a handful of salt

3 oz. thick-sliced bacon, diced

1 large onion, finely diced

1 celery stalk, finely diced

2 garlic cloves, finely chopped

1 large carrot, peeled and finely diced

2 medium potatoes, peeled and cut into 1-inch chunks

2 x 14-oz. cans peeled and chopped plum tomatoes

2 bay leaves

1 cup clam juice, or fish stock (page 43)

¼ cup fresh flatleaf parsley, chopped

sea salt and freshly ground pepper

serves 4

Meltingly delicious, ratatouille is wonderful served either as an accompaniment or as an entrée in its own right to be scooped up with crusty bread. For an authentic flavor, it is important to season each vegetable "layer" individually. Cutting the vegetables into medium-large pieces, about 1½ inches thick, helps to keep them separate.

ratatouille

Heat 3 tablespoons of the oil in a deep sauté pan with a lid. Cook the eggplant pieces over medium heat, 5 minutes each side. Add the onions and cook until soft, another 3–5 minutes. Salt lightly.

Add all the peppers and cook for 5–8 minutes more, stirring often. Turn up the heat to keep the sizzling sound going, but take care not to let it burn. Salt lightly.

Add 1 more tablespoon of the oil and the zucchini. Mix well and cook for about 5 minutes more, stirring occasionally. Salt lightly.

Add the garlic and cook for 1 minute. Add 1 more tablespoon of the oil if necessary, and the tomatoes and basil and stir well. Salt lightly. Cook for 5 minutes, then cover, lower the heat, and simmer gently for 30 minutes, checking from time to time.

Remove from the heat. This is best served at room temperature, but it still tastes nice hot. The longer you let it stand, the richer it tastes. Stir in extra basil and garlic just before serving.

2 lbs. eggplant, cut into pieces

extra virgin olive oil (see method)

2 medium onions, coarsely chopped

2 red bell peppers, halved, seeded, and cut into pieces

2 yellow bell peppers, halved, seeded, and cut into pieces

1 green bell pepper, halved, seeded, and cut into pieces

6 smallish zucchini, about 1½ lbs., halved lengthwise and sliced

4 garlic cloves, crushed

6 medium tomatoes, halved, seeded, and chopped

a small bunch of basil, coarsely chopped

coarse sea salt

to serve

a few basil leaves, finely sliced

1 garlic clove, crushed

serves 4–6

A mixture of onions, carrots, and celery sautéed in olive oil forms the base of a hearty stew with sausages and beans. This casserole is easy to prepare and doesn't take hours to cook—ideal if you want to put a nourishing meal on the table without a long hungry wait.

smoky sausage and bean casserole

Heat the oil in a heavy-based casserole dish or saucepan over high heat. Add the sausages in two batches and cook them for 4–5 minutes, turning often until cooked and an even brown on all sides. Remove them from the casserole and set aside.

Add the garlic, leek, carrot, and celery and cook for 5 minutes, stirring often. Add the tomatoes, paprika, maple syrup, thyme, beans, and 2 cups water and return the sausages to the pan.

Bring to a boil, then reduce the heat to medium and simmer for 40–45 minutes, until the sauce has thickened.

Put a slice of toasted sourdough bread on each serving plate, spoon the casserole over the top, and serve.

variation: Try replacing the sausages with 1 lb. pork neck fillet cut into 1-inch pieces. Cook the pork in batches for 4–5 minutes each batch, turning often so each piece is evenly brown. Return all the pork to the pan, as you would the sausages, and simmer for 45–50 minutes until the pork is tender.

1 tablespoon light olive oil

12 chipolata sausages

1 garlic clove, chopped

1 leek, thinly sliced

1 carrot, diced

1 celery stalk, diced

14-oz. can chopped tomatoes

1 teaspoon Spanish smoked paprika

2 tablespoons pure maple syrup

2 sprigs of fresh thyme

14-oz. can cannellini beans, drained and rinsed

to serve

toasted sourdough bread

a heavy-based casserole dish or saucepan

serves 4

Gumbos are the classic Creole stews, thick and bubbling with flavors. This one features shellfish but the dish is also often made with chicken or a variety of meats. Serve with a mound of steamed white rice.

creole gumbo

Pour 2 cups lightly salted water into a large saucepan and bring to a boil. Press in the watercress, parsley, spinach, scallions, and chard or beet greens. Cover and cook until just tender, about 5 minutes. Strain, reserving the cooking water. Chop the greens and set aside.

To make the stock, peel the shrimp and put the shells and heads, if any, into a large saucepan or casserole dish. Add the reserved cooking water, stock or water, thyme, marjoram, bay leaves, and allspice. Simmer for 15 minutes, then strain into a saucepan, return to a boil, reduce the heat, and keep warm.

Heat the butter or oil in a large casserole dish, add the flour, and sauté gently until the flour turns a hazelnut color, about 10 minutes: do not let the butter burn. Add the garlic, onion, and cayenne pepper and sauté for 2 minutes. Add the crab claws, then the reserved hot stock and the sausage, if using. Bring to a boil.

Add the clams, return to a boil, then simmer, covered, for about 15 minutes or until the clams open. Meanwhile, to prepare the okra, trim carefully around the stalk end, without cutting into the middle.

As the clams open, remove them to a plate with a slotted spoon. This will stop them overcooking. Discard any that remain closed. Add the okra to the pan. Return the reserved chopped greens to the casserole and bring to a boil. Add a dash of Tabasco sauce.

Share the seafood, okra, and greens between 4 large bowls, ladle the stock over the top, then serve with steamed white rice.

1 bunch of watercress, washed and trimmed

1 bunch of parsley, washed and trimmed

1 bunch of spinach, washed and trimmed

10 scallions, green ends only

1 bunch of chard or beet greens, washed and trimmed

1 lb. uncooked, unpeeled shrimp

4 cups chicken stock (page 41) or water

1 sprig of thyme

1 sprig of marjoram

2 bay leaves

5 whole allspice berries

1½ tablespoons butter or peanut oil

2 tablespoons all-purpose flour

2 garlic cloves, crushed

1 onion, chopped

½ teaspoon cayenne pepper

4 crab claws, preferably uncooked

8 oz. Creole smoked garlic sausage (andouille) or Polish sausage, cut into ½-inch slices (optional)

2–3 dozen clams and/or mussels, well scrubbed and debearded if necessary

8–12 medium okra

1 teaspoon Tabasco sauce

serves 4

Chunks of tender steak and puréed dried chiles make this mouthwatering chili something special. A bowlful goes down well on any occasion from a family meal to a more formal supper party.

a bowl of red

Put the beef in a medium bowl, pour the beer over, and let marinate for 30 minutes. Drain, reserving the liquid, and pat the beef dry with paper towels. Toast the chiles for 30 seconds in a dry sauté pan, then pour boiling water over and soak for 15 minutes or until soft. Drain and put in a food processor with the beer. Purée until fine and set aside.

In a large saucepan, heat 2 tablespoons of the olive oil. Season the meat and sear in batches until evenly brown. Remove from the pan and set aside. Add the remaining olive oil and sauté the onions and garlic for 5 minutes. Put the meat back in the pan and pour the chili mixture over.

Purée the tomatoes in the food processor and add to the pan. Add the cider vinegar, brown sugar, paprika, chili powder, and cumin, and season. Cook, partially covered with a lid, for 1 hour over low heat or until the meat is very tender. Add the beans in the last 5 minutes of cooking to warm through. Serve in small bowls with your choice of accompaniments, which could include steamed white rice, chopped red onion, or cilantro.

2¼ lbs. chuck eye or boneless shoulder steak, cut into 1¾-inch chunks

1 bottle beer

4 ancho chiles, stemmed and seeded

6 tablespoons extra virgin olive oil

2 large onions, roughly chopped

6 garlic cloves, finely chopped

2 x 14-oz. cans whole, peeled plum tomatoes

¼ cup cider vinegar

¼ cup brown sugar

1 tablespoon Spanish paprika (preferably pimentón)

1 tablespoon mild chili powder

3 tablespoons cumin seeds, toasted and ground

14-oz. can kidney, borlotti, or pinto beans, drained and rinsed

sea salt and freshly ground black pepper

serves 4–6

When you have nothing except risotto rice in the pantry, and a chunk of Parmesan and some butter in the refrigerator, yet feel the need for comfort and luxury, this is the risotto for you. It is pale, golden, smooth, and creamy and relies totally on the quality of these few ingredients. Real sweet, nutty Parmigiano Reggiano is best of all.

parmesan and butter risotto

Put the stock in a saucepan and keep at a gentle simmer. Melt half the butter in a large, heavy saucepan and add the onion. Cook gently for 10 minutes until the onion is soft, golden, and translucent but not brown. Add the rice and stir until well coated with the butter and heated through. Pour in the wine and boil hard until it has reduced and almost disappeared. This will remove the taste of alcohol.

Begin adding the stock, a large ladle at a time, stirring gently until each ladle has been almost absorbed by the rice. The risotto should be kept at a bare simmer throughout cooking, so don't let the rice dry out—add more stock as necessary. Continue until the rice is tender and creamy, but the grains still firm. (This should take 15–20 minutes depending on the type of rice used—check the package instructions.)

Taste and season well with salt and pepper, then stir in the remaining butter and all the Parmesan. Cover and let rest for a couple of minutes so the risotto can relax and the cheese melt, then serve immediately. You may like to add a little more stock just before serving, but don't let the risotto wait around too long or the rice will turn mushy.

about 6 cups hot chicken stock (page 41) or vegetable stock (page 43)

1 stick plus 3 tablespoons unsalted butter

1 onion, finely chopped

2⅓ cups risotto rice, preferably carnaroli

⅔ cup dry white wine

1 cup freshly grated Parmesan cheese

sea salt and freshly ground black pepper

serves 4–6

Italian mothers often put polpetti—meatballs—on the menu when they
need to provide a filling and economical meal. In this recipe, the addition
of bread crumbs is not just a thrifty measure. The bread lightens the
polpetti and also absorbs much more of the sauce and the flavorsome
oil released by the meat. Serve on Sunday night with a glass of Chianti.

beef polpetti with tomato sauce and spaghetti

Preheat the oven to 400°F.

To make the tomato sauce, put the olive oil,
garlic, onion, tomatoes, and basil in a saucepan,
season well, and bring to a boil. Reduce the heat
and simmer gently for at least 40 minutes while
you prepare the meatballs.

To make the meatballs, put the beef, bread
crumbs, eggs, Parmesan, parsley, and olive oil
in a large mixing bowl, season, and combine
with your hands. Shape the mixture into roughly
20 walnut-size balls and put in a single layer
on a baking sheet covered with foil. Roast in
the oven for 10 minutes, turn, then roast for
a further 6–7 minutes.

Put a saucepan of salted water on to boil for
the spaghetti. When it comes to a boil, drop
in the spaghetti and cook according to the
instructions on the package until al dente. Drain,
return to the pan, and add the tomato sauce
and meatballs. Stir very gently so as not to break
up the meatballs. Take out the onion wedges if
you prefer. Transfer to bowls and sprinkle with
basil and grated Parmesan to serve.

10–12 oz. spaghetti

sea salt and freshly ground black pepper

tomato sauce

¼ cup extra virgin olive oil

3 cloves garlic, peeled and thinly sliced

1 large onion, cut into wedges

2 x 14-oz. cans chopped plum tomatoes

a handful of basil, plus extra to serve

meatballs

8 oz. ground beef

1 cup fresh white bread crumbs

2 eggs

2 tablespoons freshly grated Parmesan
cheese, plus extra to serve

¼ cup chopped fresh parsley

3 tablespoons extra virgin olive oil

serves 4

Cock-a-leekie is a Scottish classic, consisting mainly of chicken wings, giblets, and barley—an easy, economical "big soup" meal. In the past, in the small stone crofts, a whole chicken and its broth would bubble deliciously in a cauldron hung in the open fireplace. Prunes add extra sweetness, but a little brown sugar could do instead.

cock-a-leekie

Put the wings, giblets, beef, whites of the leeks, thyme, parsley stalks, pearl barley, and onions in a large saucepan and add the boiling water.

Bring to a boil, reduce the heat, cover, and simmer over medium heat for 50–60 minutes. For the last 15–20 minutes, add the potatoes, prunes, and finely shredded green parts of the leeks, and cook until the potatoes are done.

Using tongs and a slotted spoon, carefully take the beef out of the saucepan and put it on a plate. Cut the beef into 4 pieces and return them to the soup. Taste and adjust the seasoning.

Ladle the soup into large bowls, sprinkle with the chopped parsley, and serve accompanied by crusty bread rolls.

variation: If you prefer, you may omit the beef altogether, but adjust the seasonings carefully to balance the flavors.

1 lb. large chicken wings

8 oz. chicken giblets, excluding liver, or extra wings

8 oz. stewing beef

1½ lbs. leeks, whites cut into ½-inch slices, green parts finely shredded

a small bunch of fresh thyme, tied with twine

a few fresh parsley stalks, plus 4 tablespoons chopped leaves, to serve

2 tablespoons pearl barley, about 1 oz.

2 onions, quartered

2 quarts boiling water

2 large potatoes, quartered

12 pitted prunes or 1 tablespoon brown sugar

sea salt and freshly ground black pepper

serves 4

Easy to prepare, these sage-crumbed pork chops are served with Irish-style colcannon. This is comfort food at its best—creamy mashed potato traditionally combined with cooked cabbage. Here, the recipe uses kale, a close relative of the cabbage. Kale is at its best in colder weather, so this dish is a good choice for crisp fall days.

sage pork chops with kale colcannon

Put the flour on a flat plate. Mix the eggs and Worcestershire sauce in a bowl and, in a separate bowl, combine the sage, bread crumbs, and Parmesan. Press a pork chop into the flour, coating the meat evenly, then dip it in the egg mixture, then press firmly to coat in the crumb mix. Repeat this process with all 4 pork chops. Transfer them to a plate and keep refrigerated until needed.

To make the colcannon, cook the kale in a large saucepan of boiling water for 5 minutes. Drain well, chop finely, and set aside.

Put the 2 tablespoons of butter in a skillet over medium heat. Add the bacon and cook for 5 minutes, stirring occasionally until the bacon turns golden. Add the scallions and cook for a further 2 minutes. Stir in the kale and remove the pan from the heat.

Put the potatoes in a large saucepan and cover with cold water. Bring to a boil and cook for 20 minutes, until soft when pierced with a skewer but not breaking apart. Drain the potatoes well and return them to the pan. Add the butter and mash well. Beat with a wooden spoon until smooth. Stir the kale mixture into the potatoes, cover, and keep warm while cooking the pork.

Heat the vegetable oil in a large skillet over medium heat. When hot, add the pork chops and cook for 6–7 minutes, so they gently sizzle in the oil and a golden crust forms. Turn over the pork chops and cook for 5 minutes on the other side. Serve with a portion of the kale colcannon.

½ cup all-purpose flour

3 eggs

2 tablespoons Worcestershire sauce

4–6 fresh sage leaves, finely chopped

1 cup fresh bread crumbs

1 cup Parmesan cheese, finely grated

4 pork chops

¼ cup vegetable oil

kale colcannon

1 lb. curly kale

1 stick butter, cut into cubes, plus 2 tablespoons for frying

2 slices of bacon, cut into strips

6–8 scallions, thinly sliced

4 large potatoes, quartered

serves 4

The shallot butter is a fancy flourish that gives this standard bar food
a real home-cooked taste. You could also serve the steaks with tarragon-
flavored béarnaise sauce (page 154) or simply Dijon mustard.

steak and fries

To make the shallot butter, put about
2 tablespoons of the butter in a saucepan and
melt over low heat. Add the shallots and cook
until softened. Add the wine, bring to a boil,
and cook until syrupy and the wine has almost
evaporated. Set aside to cool.

Put the cooled shallots, remaining butter,
tarragon, parsley, salt, and pepper in a small
food processor and blend briefly. Transfer the
mixture to a piece of parchment paper and shape
into a log. Roll up and chill until firm.

To prepare the fries, peel the potatoes and cut
into ¼-inch slices. Cut the slices into ¼-inch
strips. Put into a bowl of ice water for 5 minutes.
Drain and pat dry with paper towels.

Fill a large saucepan one-third full with the oil,
or if using a deep-fryer to the manufacturer's
recommended level. Heat the oil to 375°F or until
a cube of bread will brown in 30 seconds. Working
in batches, put 2 large handfuls of potato strips
into the frying basket, lower carefully into the oil,
and fry for about 4 minutes.

Remove and drain on paper towels. Skim any
debris off the oil, heat to the same temperature
again, then fry the strips for a second time,
about 2 minutes. Remove, drain on paper
towels, then sprinkle with salt. Keep hot in the
oven until ready to serve.

To cook the steaks, rub oil on both sides. Heat
a ridged stovetop grill pan, add the steaks and
cook for 1½–2 minutes on each side. This
produces a rare steak. For medium-rare steaks,
cook again on both sides for 2–3 minutes.
Remove from the pan, season, then serve with
rounds of the butter and the fries.

4 sirloin or rib eye steaks, about 10 oz.
each, 1 inch thick

1 tablespoon safflower oil

shallot butter

1 stick unsalted butter, softened

2 shallots, finely chopped

⅔ cup red wine

a large sprig of tarragon

several sprigs of flatleaf parsley

1 teaspoon coarse sea salt

½ teaspoon coarsely ground black
pepper

fries

1 lb. floury potatoes (for baking
and deep-frying)

safflower oil, for frying

sea salt, to serve

*a large saucepan with frying basket,
or electric deep-fryer*

serves 4

There are many burger recipes and everyone has his or her favorite—this one is very good. If you have children, they will probably enjoy helping you to shape the burger mix. Serve in a bun with onions, pickles, and sauce, and offer a simple salad of tomatoes, lettuce, and olives.

best-ever hamburgers

Put the ground steak and pork into a bowl and add the anchovies, bread crumbs, thyme, mustard, beaten egg, salt, and pepper, working it with your hands to make a nice, sticky mixture.

Shape into 6 burgers and chill for 1 hour. Cook on a preheated outdoor grill or in a lightly oiled skillet for about 4 minutes on each side. Remove from the heat and let rest for 5 minutes. Serve in a bun, with fried onions, dill pickles, and the tomato, lettuce, and olive salad, if using.

note: To make the ground meat, ask your butcher to put the beef and pork through a meat grinder. Alternatively, put it into a food processor and pulse briefly to make a slightly coarse mixture.

1½ lbs. sirloin steak, ground (see note)

2 oz. skinless pork belly, ground (see note)

8 anchovy fillets in oil, drained and finely chopped

1 cup fresh white bread crumbs

2 tablespoons chopped fresh thyme

1 tablespoon wholegrain mustard

1 extra-large egg, lightly beaten

sea salt and freshly ground black pepper

to serve

hamburger buns

sautéed onions

dill pickles

tomato, lettuce, and olive salad (optional)

serves 6

fresh from the oven

macaroni cheese · pizza margherita · meatloaf with two sauces · roast chicken with lemon, thyme, and potato stuffing · sausage and bacon toad-in-the-hole · traditional fish pie · beef and potato gratin · upside-down heirloom tomato tart · quiche lorraine · tarragon, chicken, and leek pot pie · ricotta, basil, and cherry tomato cannelloni · sticky spareribs with fresh corn salsa

Macaroni cheese, brown and bubbling on top, is the perfect "instant" food. Here, this simple family standby is given a touch of sophistication with Beaufort cheese, which has a more subtle flavor than the some cheeses. It makes a substantial meal in itself but it also works particularly well served as an accompaniment to beef stews.

macaroni cheese

Cook the macaroni in plenty of boiling, salted water according to the instructions on the package. Drain, rinse well with boiling water, and return to the empty saucepan.

Heat the milk in a saucepan and stir in the sour cream. Melt the butter in a second saucepan over medium-high heat. Stir in the flour and cook, stirring constantly for 3 minutes. Pour in the milk mixture and stir constantly until the mixture thickens. Season with salt and pepper.

Stir the milk mixture into the macaroni and taste, adding salt and pepper if necessary. Transfer to the baking dish and sprinkle with the cheese. Cook under a preheated broiler until bubbling and brown, 10–15 minutes. Serve hot.

note: Beaufort is an alpine cheese, similar to Gruyère, but with a slightly sweeter, more pronounced nutty flavor. It is becoming more widely available in supermarkets, but if you cannot find it, Emmental, Cantal, or any firm, flavorsome cheese will do. The taste will be entirely different, of course.

10 oz. thin macaroni

2 cups milk

3 tablespoons sour cream or crème fraîche

4 tablespoons unsalted butter

¼ cup all-purpose flour

coarse sea salt and freshly ground black pepper

1⅔ cups finely grated Beaufort cheese, about 7 oz. (see note)

a baking dish, 12 inches long, greased with butter

serves 6

This recipe is based on that all-time classic, the Neapolitan pizza. It should please busy working mothers because it cheats—a little—by using a ready-made pizza crust. But the richly flavored topping is authentic and made with fresh ingredients.

pizza margherita

Preheat the oven to 425°F.

To make the pizzaiola sauce, heat the oil in a shallow pan until it is almost smoking hot. Carefully add the garlic, oregano, and tomatoes (they will sputter, so stand back) and cook on high heat for 5–8 minutes. Season to taste. Press the sauce through a food mill into a bowl to remove the tomato seeds and skin.

Lightly squeeze any excess moisture out of the mozzarella, then roughly slice it.

Put the pizza crust on the baking sheet. Spread the pizzaiola sauce over the crust with the back of a spoon, leaving a ½-inch rim around the edge. Scatter with the tomatoes and season.

Put in the heated oven and bake for 5 minutes, then remove from the oven and scatter the mozzarella over the tomatoes. Return the pizza to the oven and bake for a further 15 minutes or until the crust is golden and the cheese melted but still white. Remove from the oven, scatter with the basil leaves, and drizzle with olive oil. Eat immediately.

note: These quantities make about 1¾ cups of sauce. Keep the leftovers refrigerated in a tightly sealed container to use with pasta.

2–3 oz. buffalo mozzarella or cow's milk mozzarella (*fior di latte*)

1 large ready-made pizza crust

3–4 tablespoons pizzaiola sauce (see below)

6 oz. very ripe cherry tomatoes, halved

a good handful of fresh basil leaves

extra virgin olive oil, to drizzle

sea salt and freshly ground black pepper

pizzaiola sauce (see note)

½ cup olive oil

2 garlic cloves, chopped

1 teaspoon dried oregano

2 lbs. fresh tomatoes, halved and cored

a rimless baking sheet

makes 1 medium-crust pizza, 10–14 inches

Who doesn't have nostalgic longings for meatloaf, especially the utterly delicious home-baked variety? Here meatloaf is served with two tomato sauces, one spicy for adventurous eaters.

meatloaf with two sauces

Preheat the oven to 325°F.

Line the loaf pan with the prosciutto, leaving some aside to cover the top of the finished meatloaf.

Put the chicken livers in a bowl with the pork and turkey, add the onion, eggs, bay leaves, and parsley, then season and mix well. This is best done with your hands.

Fill the prepared pan with the meat, flatten out the top, and cover with the remaining prosciutto. Cover with foil and bake in the oven for 1 hour 15 minutes. Remove and let stand for 10 minutes. Drain off any juice into a pitcher, then turn out the meatloaf onto a deep plate.

To make the tomato sauce, heat the oil and sauté the onion gently for 5 minutes. Add the garlic and cook for a further 5 minutes. Add the tomatoes and reserved meat juices, season, and simmer gently for 30 minutes, stirring frequently.

To make the spiced tomato sauce, pour half the tomato sauce mixture into another pan, add the chopped chile, and simmer for 10 minutes. Serve both sauces with the meatloaf.

12 slices prosciutto

6 oz. chicken livers, chopped

14 oz. lean pork, diced

10 oz. ground turkey or chicken

1 red onion, diced

2 eggs, beaten

3 bay leaves, torn

a bunch of flatleaf parsley, chopped

sea salt and freshly ground black pepper

tomato sauce and spiced tomato sauce

3 tablespoons olive oil

1 onion, diced

2 garlic cloves, crushed

2 x 14-oz. cans chopped tomatoes

1 red chile, chopped

a 9 x 5-inch loaf pan

serves 6

For many people, the smell of roasting chicken conjures up childhood memories of a cozy Sunday at home. It's always worth cooking a larger bird than you need because the leftovers can be used in a pilaf or to make sandwiches. You can also use the carcass to make stock, and freeze it. Three meals for the price of one bird!

roast chicken with lemon, thyme, and potato stuffing

Preheat the oven to 350°F. Lightly oil a roasting pan.

Take the chicken and carefully slide the lemon slices and bay leaves between the skin and the breast meat.

To make the stuffing, put the garlic, onion, thyme, potato, and sausage meat in a large bowl. Add the lemon zest and juice, season, and mix well. Cut any excess fat from the cavity of the chicken, then stuff the bird.

Weigh your chicken to work out the cooking time: you should allow 20 minutes per pound, plus 20 minutes extra. Put the chicken in the prepared roasting pan and lay the bacon slices over the breast. Put in the hot oven and cook for the calculated time. When the chicken is ready, remove it from the roasting pan and keep warm.

Now make the gravy. Add the flour to the pan and stir with a wooden spoon to combine with the fat and juices. Slowly pour in the chicken stock, stirring continuously to prevent lumps forming. Put the roasting pan directly over the heat and bring to a boil. When the mixture has thickened, remove it from the heat and season well. If you like a very smooth gravy, press it through a strainer with the back of a spoon.

1 medium free-range chicken

1 unwaxed lemon, thinly sliced

4 bay leaves

4 slices bacon

sea salt and freshly ground black pepper

stuffing

2 garlic cloves, crushed

1 onion, finely diced

leaves from 4 sprigs of thyme

1 large potato, coarsely grated

10 oz. sausage meat

zest and juice of 1 unwaxed lemon

gravy

2 tablespoons all-purpose flour

2 cups chicken stock (page 41)

serves 4

Simple, tasty, and low-cost—the humble toad-in-the-hole makes a great midweek supper dish. This takes little time to prepare and will be popular with all the family. You can serve it with any vegetables you like, but mashed potato and your favorite gravy are particularly good.

sausage and bacon toad-in-the-hole

Preheat the oven to 425°F.

Put the flour in a mixing bowl and make a well in the center. Beat the eggs, milk, seasoning, and a generous ½ cup water together and pour into the well. Stir carefully with a wooden spoon until you have a smooth batter. Let rest for 30 minutes.

Grease a large roasting pan or 4–6 individual dishes and place in the oven.

Wrap the bacon around the sausages and place in the hot roasting pan or dishes. Add the onion, then pour in the batter. Return to the oven and bake for 30 minutes without opening the door. The batter should be light and well risen.

1½ cups all-purpose flour

2 eggs

⅔ cup milk

8 slices bacon

2 lbs. sausages

2 red onions, cut into wedges

sea salt and freshly ground black pepper

serves 4–6

Nothing beats a steaming, creamy fish pie—light but satisfying. The hint of mustard and the addition of hard-cooked eggs lift this from an ordinary supper dish to a fantastic winner of a pie. If you use finnan haddie, try to buy the pale yellow (undyed) fish.

traditional fish pie

Preheat the oven to 400°F.

Put the milk in a wide saucepan, heat just to boiling point, then add the fish. Turn off the heat and leave the fish to poach until opaque—do not overcook.

Meanwhile, melt 1¼ sticks of the butter in another saucepan, then stir in the mustard and flour. Remove from the heat and strain the poaching liquid into the pan.

Arrange the fish and eggs in a shallow pie dish or casserole.

Return the pan to the heat and, beating vigorously to smooth out any lumps, bring the mixture to a boil. Season to taste. (Take care: if you are using smoked fish, it may be salty enough.) Pour the sauce into the casserole and mix carefully with the fish and eggs.

Cook the potatoes in boiling salted water until soft, then drain. Return to the pan. Melt the remaining 1½ sticks butter in a small saucepan. Reserve ¼ cup of this butter and stir the remainder into the potatoes. Mash well and season. Spoon the mixture carefully over the sauced fish, brush with the reserved butter, and transfer to the oven. Cook for 20 minutes, or until nicely brown.

note: If you can't find finnan haddie, you can sprinkle 4 oz. smoked salmon, finely sliced, over the poached fresh haddock just before adding the sauce.

2 cups milk

1½ lbs. finnan haddie or fresh haddock, skinned

2¾ sticks unsalted butter

1 tablespoon dry mustard powder

¼ cup all-purpose flour

2 hard-cooked eggs, peeled and quartered

2 lbs. floury potatoes

sea salt and freshly ground black pepper

serves 4

The traditional recipe calls for leftover cooked beef, so if you had a Sunday roast, this pie is perfect for Monday supper. Otherwise, ground beef that has been well seasoned and cooked in a splash of wine comes a close second. Serve with a fruity red wine.

beef and potato gratin

Preheat the oven to 400°F.

To make the purée, put the potatoes and bay leaf in a saucepan of cold water. Bring to a boil, add salt, and cook until tender. Drain.

Put the potatoes in a large bowl and mash coarsely with a wooden spoon. Using an electric whisk, gradually add the milk and butter, beating until the mixture is smooth. Add salt and beat well. If the potatoes are very dry, add more milk. Taste, then add more butter and/or salt as necessary and set aside.

Heat the butter in a skillet, add the onions, and cook over high heat until just brown, 3–5 minutes. Add the garlic, beef, and bacon and cook until almost completely brown. Add the wine and cook until almost evaporated. Stir in the parsley, thyme leaves, and tomato paste. Season to taste.

Spread the beef mixture over the baking dish and level with a spoon. Spread with the potatoes. Sprinkle with the cheese and bake in the oven until golden, about 25–30 minutes.

3 tablespoons unsalted butter or 2 tablespoons safflower oil

2 onions, chopped

2 garlic cloves, crushed

1½ lbs. ground beef

3 slices bacon, finely chopped

½ cup dry white wine

a handful of fresh flatleaf parsley, chopped

a fresh thyme sprig, leaves stripped

2 tablespoons tomato paste

2 oz. freshly grated Cheddar cheese, about ¾ cup

sea salt and freshly ground black pepper

potato purée

4 lbs. potatoes

1 bay leaf

1 cup hot milk

1 stick unsalted butter, diced

sea salt

a baking dish, about 12 inches long

serves 4–6

What exactly is an heirloom tomato? Opinions vary and include classification based on the age of the seed. One of the nicest explanations is that an heirloom is a variety that has been nurtured and handed down from generation to generation within a family. Choose a variety that stays fairly firm when cooked.

upside-down heirloom tomato tart

Preheat the oven to 425°F.

Put the oil, capers, and rosemary in a heatproof nonstick skillet. Put over high heat and when the capers start to sizzle add the tomatoes, firmly pressing them down in a single layer in the skillet. Cook for 3–4 minutes to allow the tomatoes to sizzle and soften.

Place the sheet of pastry dough over the tomatoes, folding in the corners, being careful not to press down on the tomatoes. Transfer the skillet to the preheated oven and cook for 18–20 minutes, until the pastry is puffed and golden. Remove the skillet from the oven and let the tart rest for a couple of minutes.

Place a serving plate that is larger than the skillet upside-down on top of the skillet and quickly flip the skillet over so the tart falls onto the plate. Sprinkle with cracked black pepper and a drizzle of olive oil and cut into 4 wedges to serve.

variation: Make a roasted tomato sauce using prime summer tomatoes. Cut 6 medium tomatoes in half and place them on a baking sheet, cut side up, with 1 sliced red onion, 3 sliced garlic cloves, 2 tablespoons olive oil, and ½ teaspoon each of sea salt and white sugar sprinkled over. Bake in a preheated oven at 325°F for 1½ hours. Remove from the oven and process in a food processor with 3–4 fresh basil leaves, until you have a chunky sauce. Serve with pasta of your choice.

2 tablespoons light olive oil

2 teaspoons small capers, rinsed if salted

10–12 fresh rosemary needles

3 ripe tomatoes, thickly sliced

12-oz. sheet ready-rolled puff pastry dough, defrosted if frozen

cracked black pepper

extra virgin olive oil, for drizzling

a nonstick, heatproof skillet, 8–9 inches diameter

serves 4, as a starter

This classic tart is the forerunner of many versions of quiche. Made with light, crumbly shortcrust pastry dough filled with the best ingredients, this simplest of dishes is food fit for the gods—and a family favorite, of course. A touch of grated Gruyère adds interest to the flavor.

quiche lorraine

Preheat the oven to 400°F.

To make the pastry dough, sift the flour and salt into a large bowl. Rub in the shortening and butter with your fingers until the mixture looks like bread crumbs. Lightly mix in the water with a knife.

Roll out the dough thinly on a lightly floured work surface and press it into the tart pan. Prick the base, and chill or freeze for 15 minutes. Then line the base with aluminum foil or parchment paper, fill with baking beans, and bake blind in the oven for 10–12 minutes.

Remove the pie crust from the oven and remove the foil and baking beans. Brush the crust with a little beaten egg and return to the oven for another 5–10 minutes.

Heat a nonstick skillet and sauté the bacon until brown and crisp, then drain on paper towels. Scatter over the pie crust.

Put the eggs and cream into a bowl, beat well, and season with salt, pepper, and nutmeg to taste. Carefully pour the mixture over the bacon and sprinkle with the Gruyère.

Bake for 25 minutes or until just set and golden brown. Serve warm or at room temperature.

8 oz. bacon, chopped, or cubed prosciutto

5 eggs

¾ cup heavy cream or crème fraîche

freshly grated nutmeg, to taste

½ cup Gruyère cheese, grated, about 2 oz.

sea salt and freshly ground black pepper

shortcrust pastry dough

2 cups all-purpose flour

a pinch of salt

4½ tablespoons vegetable shortening or lard, chilled and diced

6 tablespoons unsalted butter, chilled and cubed

2–3 tablespoons chilled water

a little beaten egg

a tart pan, 9 inches diameter

baking beans

serves 4–6

This will be a popular choice for fall meals. No one needs persuading to eat chicken pie—and it celebrates the season with freshly grown leeks, at their very best in the cooler weather.

tarragon, chicken, and leek pot pie

Preheat the oven to 350°F.

Heat half the butter in a skillet over high heat. When it sizzles, cook the chicken in two batches for 2–3 minutes, turning often to brown the pieces all over. Transfer to a bowl.

Add the remaining butter to the skillet and cook the leeks over medium heat for 2 minutes. Cover with a lid, reduce the heat, and cook for 2–3 minutes, until really softened.

Return the chicken to the skillet and increase the heat to high. Sprinkle the flour into the skillet and cook for 2 minutes, stirring constantly to coat the chicken and leeks. Gradually add the stock, stirring all the time. Bring to a boil, then stir in the cream, tarragon, and parsley. Season well. Reduce the heat and simmer until thickened, about 1 minute. Remove from the heat and let cool. Spoon into an ovenproof pie dish.

To make the pastry dough, put the flour, butter, and a pinch of salt in a food processor and process for a few seconds. With the motor running, add the sour cream, half the beaten egg, and 1–2 tablespoons cold water, until the dough comes together. Roll into a ball, wrap in plastic wrap, and refrigerate for 30 minutes.

Place the dough between two pieces of waxed paper and roll out to a thickness of ¼ inch. Drape the dough over the pie, leaving the edges to overhang. Cut slits in the top of the pie and press gently around the edges with a fork. Brush the remaining beaten egg over the top. Put the pie dish on a baking sheet and cook in the preheated oven for 30 minutes, until the pastry is golden.

3 tablespoons butter

1 ½ lbs. chicken thigh fillets, cut into bite-size pieces

4 medium leeks (white parts only), thickly sliced

3 tablespoons all-purpose flour

1 cup chicken stock (page 41)

1 cup light cream

2 tablespoons finely chopped fresh tarragon

2 tablespoons roughly chopped flatleaf parsley

sea salt and freshly ground black pepper

pastry dough

1 ½ cups all-purpose flour

2 tablespoons butter

2 tablespoons sour cream

1 egg, lightly beaten

3-quart ovenproof pie dish

serves 4

You can assemble this the day before, refrigerate it, put in the oven at the last moment, and then wait for the family's applause! It's fine to vary the type of cheese, as long as it is a soft one.

ricotta, basil, and cherry tomato cannelloni

Preheat the oven to 425°F.

Cut 8 oz. of the whole cherry tomatoes in half and set aside for the top.

Heat the oil in a skillet, add the uncut tomatoes (they will sputter a little), and cover tightly. Cook over high heat, shaking the skillet occasionally, for 5 minutes until the tomatoes start to break down. Uncover and stir in the oregano, sugar, salt, and pepper. Set aside.

Soften the cheese in a bowl and beat in the pesto. Put all the sheets of lasagne on a work surface and spread the cheese mixture evenly over them. Put 2 tomato slices on each sheet, season well, and roll up from the narrow side like a jelly roll. Spoon half the tomato sauce in the bottom of the baking dish. Put the pasta rolls on top of the sauce, then spoon over the remaining sauce. Dot with the reserved cherry tomato halves and cover with aluminum foil.

Bake in the oven for 25–30 minutes. Uncover, sprinkle with the Parmesan, and bake or broil for a further 10 minutes until beginning to brown. Remove from the oven and let stand for 10 minutes before serving.

Top with basil and serve with a crisp green salad.

note: If using dried lasagne sheets, cook in boiling salted water according to the package instructions. Carefully lift them out of the water and drain in a colander. Transfer to a bowl of cold water. Lift out and drain each sheet before spreading with the cheese mixture.

1 ½ lbs. ripe cherry tomatoes, whole, plus 12 oz. vine-ripened tomatoes, thinly sliced (you need 24 slices)

⅓ cup extra virgin olive oil

2 teaspoons dried oregano

2 teaspoons sugar

10 oz. ricotta cheese

⅓ cup fresh pesto (page 164)

12 sheets of fresh lasagne (see note)

3 tablespoons freshly grated Parmesan cheese

a handful of basil leaves

sea salt and freshly ground black pepper

green salad, to serve

a baking dish, 10 x 8 inches, lightly oiled

serves 4

These lip-smackingly good ribs are basted and then left in a full-flavored marinade overnight. Teenagers love them as finger food! It is important to use fresh corn for the salsa and shuck it just before cooking. So don't buy cobs smothered with plastic. Instead, look for summer-ripened ones still in their silky skins.

sticky spareribs with fresh corn salsa

To make the marinade, put the maple syrup, sugar, vinegar, fish sauce, garlic, and chiles in a saucepan and bring to a boil, stirring constantly, until the sugar has dissolved. Simmer for 10 minutes until the mixture has thickened. Remove from the heat and let cool. Put the ribs in a large flat dish with the marinade, cover, and refrigerate overnight, turning the ribs often.

Preheat the oven to 400°F.

To make the salsa, heat 1 tablespoon of the olive oil in a skillet over high heat. Add the corn and cook for 4–5 minutes, stirring often, until the kernels start to turn golden. Add the onion and chile and stir for 1 minute to soften the onions a little. Remove from the heat and let cool. Stir in the remaining olive oil, vinegar, cilantro, and mint.

Put the ribs and marinade in a single layer on a baking sheet and cook in the preheated oven for 30 minutes. Turn the ribs and return them to the oven for a further 10–15 minutes. (If the ribs start to stick to the sheet in the final few minutes of cooking, reduce the temperature to 350°F.) Serve with the salsa and any remaining marinade spooned over.

1 cup pure maple syrup

½ cup packed brown sugar

1½ cups cider vinegar

½ cup Thai fish sauce

2 garlic cloves, crushed

10–12 large dried red chiles (Kashmiri)

8 long spareribs, ideally 4–6 inches

corn salsa

3 tablespoons light olive oil

1½ cups fresh corn kernels (from 2 ears), shucked

1 small red onion, chopped

1 large red chile, seeded and finely chopped

2 tablespoons red wine vinegar

1 small bunch of fresh cilantro, chopped

1 large handful of fresh mint leaves, chopped

serves 4

sweet temptations

blueberry sour cream pancakes with maple syrup pecans • breakfast doughnuts • scones with clotted cream and strawberry jam • bird's nest cupcakes • cranberry and bittersweet chocolate brownies • chocolate fudge cookies • bread and butter puddings • sticky toffee pudding • old english trifle • chocolate mousse • crème caramel • new york cheesecake • mississippi mud pie • strawberry shortcake • blackberry crumble • dusky apple pie • banana splits with hot fudge sauce • raspberries-and-cream layer cake • carrot and walnut cake with cream cheese frosting

A delicious treat with an all-American flavor, these pancakes will disappear as fast as you can put them on the table. You can make the pancakes with either fresh or frozen berries. The frozen ones take slightly longer to cook and so are less likely to burn.

blueberry sour cream pancakes with maple syrup pecans

Preheat the oven to 400°F.

To make the maple syrup pecans, spread the nuts over a baking sheet and cook in the preheated oven for 5 minutes until lightly toasted. Simmer the maple syrup in a small saucepan for 3 minutes. Remove from the heat and stir in the pecans and butter.

To make the pancakes, sift the flour, baking powder, salt, and sugar into a bowl. Put the egg yolks, sour cream, milk, and butter into a second bowl and beat well, then add the flour mixture all at once and beat until smooth. Put the egg whites into a clean bowl and beat until soft peaks form. Fold them gently into the batter, then fold in the blueberries. Do not overmix—a few lumps of flour and egg white don't matter.

Heat the prepared griddle over medium heat. Reduce the heat. Pour 3 tablespoons of batter into the pan and cook in batches of 3–4 for 1–2 minutes over very low heat to avoid burning the blueberries, until small bubbles begin to appear on top and the underside is golden brown. Turn them over and cook the other side for 1 minute. Transfer to a plate and keep them warm in a low oven while you cook the remainder.

Serve with good vanilla ice cream and the maple syrup pecans.

1½ cups all-purpose flour

2 teaspoons baking powder

1 teaspoon salt

¼ cup sugar

2 eggs, separated

1 cup sour cream

⅔ cup milk

4 tablespoons unsalted butter, melted and cooled

8 oz. blueberries, fresh or frozen

vanilla ice cream, to serve

maple syrup pecans

4 oz. pecan halves

1 cup pure maple syrup

4 tablespoons unsalted butter

a baking sheet

a flat griddle pan or skillet, preheated and lightly greased

makes 8–10 pancakes

Doughnuts with coffee are a time-honored midmorning snack, but made to this recipe they are substantial enough to eat for breakfast. Rather than a yeast dough, these use mashed floury potatoes for speed and flavor. They are best eaten freshly made and still warm.

breakfast doughnuts

Mix the flour with the salt, spices, baking soda, and sugar in a large bowl. Rub in the butter with the tips of your fingers until the mixture looks like crumbs.

Add the mashed potatoes, work in briefly, then work in the eggs and enough of the buttermilk to make a soft, cookie-like dough. If the dough feels very sticky, work in extra flour, adding 1 tablespoon at a time.

Turn out the dough onto a lightly floured work surface and knead for a few seconds until it is just smooth. Roll it out ½ inch thick, then cut out rounds using the larger cutter. Stamp out the center of each round with the smaller cutter.

Re-roll the trimmings and center circles, then cut out more rings.

Fill a large frying pan one-third full with the oil (or a deep-fryer to the manufacturer's recommended level). Heat the oil to 350°F, or until a small cube of bread turns brown in 40 seconds. Fry the doughnuts 2 or 3 at a time, turning them frequently until quite brown and cooked through, about 4 minutes. Remove from the oil with a slotted spoon and drain well on paper towels.

Mix the cinnamon sugar ingredients together, sprinkle over the doughnuts, then serve warm with coffee.

Best eaten within 24 hours.

3 cups all-purpose flour

¼ teaspoon sea salt

½ teaspoon ground ginger

½ teaspoon ground cinnamon

½ teaspoon freshly grated nutmeg

1½ teaspoons baking soda

1 cup sugar

3 tablespoons unsalted butter, diced

1 cup firmly packed, very smooth mashed potatoes (page 31)

2 eggs, beaten

1 cup buttermilk (or a mixture of half plain yogurt and half lowfat milk)

vegetable oil, for deep-frying

cinnamon sugar

2 tablespoons sugar

1 teaspoon ground cinnamon

a large frying pan or saucepan, or an electric deep-fryer

3-inch round plain cookie cutter

1-inch round plain cookie cutter

makes 12 doughnuts

Traditionally served with clotted cream and rich, fruity jam, these classic scones are a must for the family tea table. Some people put the jam on first, followed by a dollop of cream; others argue for putting the cream on first. For real luxury, use homemade strawberry jam (page 173).

scones with clotted cream and strawberry jam

Preheat the oven to 425°F.

Put the flour, baking powder, and sugar in a food processor and pulse to combine. Add the butter and process for about 20 seconds until the mixture resembles fine bread crumbs. Transfer to a large bowl and make a well in the center.

Beat together the egg and milk in another bowl, reserving 1 tablespoon of the mixture in a separate bowl. Pour most of the remaining liquid into the flour mixture and bring together into a soft dough using a fork. If there are still dry crumbs, add a little more of the liquid. Turn out onto a lightly floured surface and knead briefly until smooth. Work in a little more flour if the mixture is sticky. Gently pat or roll out the dough to about 1 inch thick and cut out rounds using the cookie cutter, pressing the trimmings together to make more scones.

Arrange the scones on a greased baking sheet, spacing them slightly apart, and brush the tops with the reserved egg and milk mixture. Bake for about 8 minutes, or until risen and golden. Transfer to a wire rack to cool slightly. Serve warm with clotted cream and strawberry jam.

1¾ cups self-rising flour

1 teaspoon baking powder

2 tablespoons sugar

3 tablespoons plus 1 teaspoon unsalted butter, chilled and diced

1 egg

⅓ cup milk

to serve

clotted cream

good-quality strawberry jam

a 2-inch cookie cutter

makes 10–12 scones

Children love these little chocolate nests with pretty pastel-colored eggs nestling inside. They're easy to make and kids will have a great time helping to decorate them—perfect if you're looking for a fun activity on a rainy afternoon. The eggs make them a good choice for a sweet treat at Easter time, but you can enjoy them at any season.

bird's nest cupcakes

Preheat the oven to 350°F.

Beat the butter and sugar together in a bowl until pale and fluffy, then beat in the eggs, one at a time. Sift the flour and cocoa powder into the mixture and fold in, then stir in the milk.

Spoon the mixture into the paper liners and bake in the preheated oven for 18 minutes until risen and a skewer inserted in the center comes out clean. Transfer to a wire rack to cool.

To decorate, put the mascarpone, confectioners' sugar, and cocoa powder in a bowl and beat together until smooth and creamy. Pop a dollop of frosting on top of each cupcake.

Using a vegetable peeler, make some chocolate shavings and arrange them on top of the frosting to create 12 little bird's nests. Finish off with three eggs in the center of each nest.

1 stick unsalted butter, at room temperature

½ cup sugar

2 eggs

1 cup self-rising flour

1½ tablespoons unsweetened cocoa powder

2 tablespoons milk

to decorate

⅔ cup mascarpone

⅓ cup confectioners' sugar, sifted

1 tablespoon unsweetened cocoa powder

chocolate, for shavings

36 sugar-coated chocolate eggs (about 3½ oz.)

a 12-cup cupcake pan, lined with paper liners

makes 12 cupcakes

The sharpness of dried cranberries balances the sweetness of this bittersweet chocolate brownie, and the tangy grated orange zest lifts the richness. These sophisticated brownies will keep moist for up to 5 days, though there's not much chance of them staying uneaten that long!

cranberry and bittersweet chocolate brownies

Preheat the oven to 350°F.

Break up the chocolate and put it in a heatproof mixing bowl with the butter. Set the bowl over a saucepan of steaming water and melt gently, stirring frequently. Remove the bowl from the pan and let cool until needed.

Beat the eggs until frothy using an electric mixer or whisk. Add the sugar and orange zest and beat until the mixture becomes very thick and mousse-like. Beat in the melted chocolate.

Sift the flour onto the mixture and stir in. When everything is thoroughly combined stir in the dried cranberries. Transfer the mixture to the prepared pan and spread evenly.

Bake in the preheated oven for about 25 minutes or until a skewer inserted halfway between the sides and the center comes out just clean. Remove the pan from the oven.

Let cool before removing from the pan and cutting into 20 pieces. Store in an airtight container and eat within 5 days.

7 oz. good bittersweet chocolate

1¾ sticks unsalted butter, diced

3 extra-large eggs

1 cup less 1 tablespoon sugar

grated zest of 1 medium unwaxed orange

1½ cups all-purpose flour

⅔ cup dried cranberries

a brownie pan, 8 x 10 inches, greased and base-lined

makes 20 brownies

This very quick recipe uses a food processor. Semisweet chocolate gives the cookies a rich flavor. They are excellent for serving with a good vanilla ice cream and can be enjoyed at any time with a cup of coffee.

chocolate fudge cookies

Preheat the oven to 350°F.

Put both the sugars in a food processor. Add the pieces of chocolate, then process until the mixture has a sandy texture.

Add the pieces of butter, flour, baking powder, and egg and process until the mixture comes together to make a firm dough. Carefully remove from the machine.

Lightly flour your hands and roll the dough into about 20 walnut-size balls. Arrange them, spaced well apart, on the prepared sheets.

Bake in the preheated oven for 12–15 minutes until firm.

Let cool on the sheets for 2 minutes, then transfer to wire racks to cool completely.

Store in an airtight container and eat within 5 days or freeze for up to a month.

variation: Remove the dough from the processor and work in ½ cup pecan pieces, then shape and bake the cookies as above.

⅓ cup sugar

½ cup firmly packed light brown sugar

5 oz. good semisweet chocolate, broken up

1 stick unsalted butter, chilled and diced

1¼ cups all-purpose flour

½ teaspoon baking powder

1 extra-large egg, lightly beaten

several baking sheets, greased

makes about 20

Bread and butter pudding is a childhood favorite for many people—but grown-ups love it, too. This simple dish is enjoying something of a revival at the moment. There are various ways of making it, and here slices of brioche bread are used instead of ordinary bread. Taking less than 20 minutes to cook, this pudding is served in individual dishes.

bread and butter puddings

Preheat the oven to 350°F.

Put the milk, cream, vanilla extract, and 3 tablespoons of the sugar into a saucepan and heat until the sugar dissolves.

Put the eggs into a bowl, beat well, stir in 2–3 tablespoons of the hot milk mixture to warm the eggs, then stir in the remainder of the hot milk.

Lightly toast the slices of brioche and cut into quarters. Divide between the prepared dishes and sprinkle with the raisins.

Pour in the custard, grate a little nutmeg over the top, then sprinkle with the remaining sugar. Bake for 18–20 minutes, or until firm. Let cool a little, then serve warm.

1¼ cups milk

1¼ cups heavy cream

½ teaspoon pure vanilla extract

¼ cup sugar

3 eggs

6 thick slices of brioche bread

2 oz. golden raisins, ⅓ cup

1 whole nutmeg

6 individual dishes, 1 cup each, well greased

serves 6

This is the sort of gloriously sticky pudding that really does leave happy memories. It can be mixed, baked in the oven, and placed on the table in under an hour. The toffee sauce is also good poured over ice cream.

sticky toffee pudding

Preheat the oven to 350°F.

To make the pudding, put the dates and the boiling water in a small saucepan or heatproof bowl, then stir in the baking soda and let soak until needed.

Put the butter in a mixing bowl or the bowl of an electric mixer. Add the sugar and vanilla extract and beat until very well combined (the mixture won't look soft and fluffy like a pound cake mix).

Pour a little of the beaten egg into the mixing bowl and beat well. Keep on adding the eggs, a little at a time, then beating well, until all the eggs have been used up.

Sift the flour and baking powder into the bowl. Stir gently a few times to half-mix in the flour, then pour the date and water mixture into the bowl. Carefully mix the whole lot together to make a runny batter.

Pour the batter into the prepared baking dish and bake for 40–45 minutes, or until golden brown. A skewer inserted into the center should come out clean. If not, give the pudding another 5 minutes in the oven before testing again.

While the pudding is baking, make the toffee sauce. Put the sugar, butter, and cream in a small saucepan. Set the pan over low heat and heat gently, stirring now and then until melted, smooth, and hot. Remove the pudding from the oven and serve warm with the hot toffee sauce. Any leftover pudding and sauce can be gently reheated and served again. Eat within 2 days.

1 cup stoned dates, chopped

1¼ cups boiling water

1 teaspoon baking soda

4 tablespoons unsalted butter, softened

¾ cup sugar

½ teaspoon pure vanilla extract

2 extra-large eggs, at room temperature, beaten

1⅔ cups all-purpose flour

1 teaspoon baking powder

toffee sauce

⅔ cup firm-packed soft dark brown sugar

4 tablespoons unsalted butter

1 cup light cream

an ovenproof baking dish, about 3 pints capacity, greased

makes 1 large pudding

Ladyfingers soaked in sherry and topped with fruit, homemade egg custard, and cream, create this delicious trifle, which everyone will adore. Try canned apricots instead of peaches or 12–14 oz. thinly sliced Madeira cake instead of the ladyfingers.

old english trifle

Spread the top of each ladyfinger with jam, then arrange them over the base of the serving bowl, covering the base completely. Sprinkle the crushed amaretti evenly over the top.

Drain the peaches, reserving the juice. Mix together the peach juice and sherry, then pour evenly over the ladyfingers and amaretti. Arrange the peaches in an even layer over the top. Cover and refrigerate.

Meanwhile, put the cornstarch in a heatproof bowl, add 3 tablespoons of the milk and blend together with a whisk until smooth. Add the egg yolks, sugar, and vanilla extract and beat together to mix. Set aside.

Pour the remaining milk in a saucepan and heat gently until almost boiling. Pour the hot milk onto the egg yolk mixture, beating constantly. Return the mixture to the pan, then cook gently, stirring continuously, until the mixture thickens enough to coat the back of a wooden spoon. Do not allow the mixture to boil as it may curdle.

Remove the pan from the heat and pour the custard into a heatproof bowl. Cover the surface of the hot custard with a piece of parchment paper (to prevent a skin forming) and let cool completely.

Spoon the cold custard over the peach layer. Lightly whip the cream until it forms soft peaks, then spread cream over the custard, covering it completely. Cover and refrigerate for 3–4 hours before serving. Sprinkle the cream with the slivered almonds, then serve.

12 ladyfingers

½ cup raspberry jam

4½ oz. amaretti, lightly crushed

15 oz. canned sliced peaches in fruit juice

6 tablespoons sherry

1 tablespoon cornstarch

2⅓ cups whole milk

4 egg yolks

¼ cup sugar

1 teaspoon pure vanilla extract

1¼ cups heavy cream

⅓ cup slivered almonds

a deep glass serving bowl

serves 8

This is very easy to make and ideal for entertaining, since it should be made one day in advance. It is also deceptively rich, thanks to the egg yolks, which can be reduced in quantity or omitted altogether. It is important to use good-quality chocolate, but anything over 70 percent cocoa solids will be too strongly flavored.

chocolate mousse

Put the chocolate in a heatproof bowl and melt gently over a pan of steaming water. Alternatively, melt in the microwave on HIGH for 40 seconds, then stir and repeat until almost completely melted. Stir the butter into the melted chocolate. Using the tip of a small knife, scrape the small black seeds from the vanilla bean into the chocolate. Add the egg yolks, stir, and set the mixture aside.

Using an electric mixer, beat the egg whites and salt until foaming. Continue beating and add the sugar. Beat on high until glossy and firm.

Carefully fold the whites into the chocolate with a rubber spatula until no more white specks can be seen.

Transfer the mousse to serving dishes and refrigerate for at least 6 hours, but overnight is best. To serve, add a blob of whipped cream on top of each mousse, or offer the cream in a separate bowl for people to help themselves.

7 oz. bittersweet chocolate, broken into pieces

2 tablespoons unsalted butter, cut into small pieces

1 vanilla bean, split lengthwise with a small sharp knife

3 eggs, separated

a pinch of salt

2 tablespoons sugar

whipped cream, to serve (optional)

serves 4

Preparation of crème caramel is simple, and it is equally easy to eat!
There is a knack to turning out professional-looking custards. After baking,
leave them in the bain-marie for 15 minutes before removing them. Then
run a knife around the inside edge of each ramekin, hold an upturned
plate over the top, and flip over to release a perfect custard.

crème caramel

Preheat the oven to 350°F.

Put the milk, vanilla bean, and its seeds in a
saucepan over medium heat and bring just to
a boil. Immediately remove from the heat, cover,
and let stand while you make the caramel.

To make the caramel, put ½ cup of the sugar, a
pinch of salt, and ¼ cup water in a small, heavy
saucepan, preferably with a pouring lip. Heat
until the sugar turns a deep caramel color, then
remove from the heat. When it stops sizzling,
pour carefully into the ramekins. Take care not
to let the caramel come into contact with your
skin; it is very hot. Set the ramekins in a roasting
pan and add enough boiling water to the pan to
come halfway up the sides of the ramekins—this
is called a bain-marie. Set aside.

Add the remaining sugar and another pinch of
salt to the saucepan of warm milk and stir until
dissolved. Remove the vanilla bean.

Put the eggs in another bowl and beat until
smooth. Pour the warm milk into the eggs and
stir well. Ladle into the ramekins.

Carefully transfer the roasting pan with the
ramekins to the preheated oven and bake until
the custard has set and a knife inserted into the
middle comes out clean, about 20–25 minutes.
Serve at room temperature either in their
ramekins or inverted onto a plate so the caramel
forms a pool of sweet sauce round the custard.

3 cups whole milk

1 vanilla bean, split lengthwise with
a small sharp knife

¾ cup plus 2 tablespoons sugar

5 extra-large eggs

salt

8 ramekin dishes

a roasting pan to hold the ramekins

serves 8

Traditional cheesecakes are often served with a thick fruit sauce on top. This one is so dense and creamy that it really needs no embellishment. If you like, simply smother the top with a selection of fresh soft fruit such as raspberries, strawberries, blueberries, or cherries.

new york cheesecake

Preheat the oven to 275°F.

Crush the graham crackers in a food processor then add the melted butter and mix well. Press the mixture firmly into the cake pan. Bake for 5 minutes, remove, and let cool. Grease the sides of the pan above the crust.

In a large bowl, beat the cream cheese and sugar with an electric beater. Add the lemon peel and juice, sour cream, and vanilla extract. Mix until smooth and add the eggs one at a time until well combined. Put the flour in last and mix again. Pour the mixture into the cake pan. Bake for 70 minutes until it is firm and the top is turning light golden. Let sit in the oven with the door open until cool (about 2 hours), then refrigerate for at least 6 hours or overnight. Place your favorite fresh fruit on top and serve.

7 oz. graham crackers or chocolate wafers

4 tablespoons melted butter

1 lb. 14 oz. cream cheese

1 cup sugar

grated peel and freshly squeezed juice of 1 unwaxed lemon

1 cup sour cream

2 tablespoons pure vanilla extract

5 eggs

¼ cup all-purpose flour

a selection of fresh soft fruit

a springform cake pan, about 8 inches diameter

serves 8–10

This famous pie hails from the south—it is supposed to look like the thick, dark, muddy waters of the Mississippi delta. It is very easy to make and is perfect for sharing with family and friends.

mississippi mud pie

Preheat the oven to 350°F.

To make the base, put the graham crackers into a food processor and process until fine crumbs form. Alternatively, put the crackers into a plastic bag and crush with a rolling pin. Transfer the crumbs to a mixing bowl.

Put the butter and chocolate into a heatproof bowl set over a small saucepan of steaming but not boiling water and melt gently (do not let the base of the bowl touch the water). Stir occasionally, until smooth. Remove from the heat, then stir into the cracker crumbs. When well mixed, transfer to the prepared cake pan and, using the back of a spoon, press onto the base and about halfway up the sides of the pan. Chill while making the filling.

To make the filling, melt the chocolate and butter as above. Remove from the heat and let cool.

Put the eggs and sugars into a large mixing bowl and, using an electric beater or mixer, beat until thick and foamy. Beat in the cream followed by the melted chocolate. Pour the mixture into the cookie crust and bake in the preheated oven for about 45 minutes until just firm. Let cool for a few minutes, then remove from the pan.

To make the chocolate cream, put the cream into a mixing bowl, then sift the cocoa and confectioners' sugar on top and stir gently with a wooden spoon until blended. Cover and chill for 2 hours.

Serve at room temperature with the chocolate cream. The pie can be made up to 2 days in advance. Keep it well covered in the refrigerator and remove 30 minutes before serving.

8 oz. graham crackers

4 tablespoons unsalted butter

2 oz. bittersweet chocolate, finely chopped

filling

6 oz. bittersweet chocolate, chopped

1½ sticks unsalted butter, diced

4 extra-large eggs, beaten

½ cup firmly packed light brown sugar

½ cup firmly packed dark brown sugar

1¾ cups heavy cream

chocolate cream

⅔ cup heavy cream, well chilled

3 tablespoons unsweetened cocoa powder

⅓ cup confectioners' sugar

a springform cake pan, 9 inches diameter, well greased

serves 8

This luxurious pudding has a shell of rich but light cake—known as genoise—piled with chantilly cream and fruit. The secret of getting genoise to rise is to beat a lot of air into the mixture, so turn your mixer to high and keep it going for at least 10–15 minutes. Don't wait for a party to try this recipe. Just make it whenever the family deserves a treat.

strawberry shortcake

Preheat the oven to 350°F.

To make the genoise, put the eggs and sugar in a bowl and beat with an electric mixer until light and fluffy. Using a spatula or whisk, fold in the flour until just blended. Transfer the mixture to the prepared pan and bake in the preheated oven until golden, about 20–25 minutes. Remove from the oven, unmold after 5 minutes, and let cool on a wire rack.

To prepare the sugar syrup, mix the sugar and 5 tablespoons water in a small saucepan. Bring just to a boil and stir to dissolve the sugar. Remove from the heat and stir in the brandy. Set aside.

Put the strawberries in a bowl with a squeeze of lemon juice. Add 1 tablespoon of the sugar and toss to coat. Set aside. To make the chantilly cream, mix the remaining sugar and the cream in a bowl. Beat until it holds stiff peaks. Set aside.

Put the genoise on a board and, using a serrated knife, trace a circle around the top of the cake, about ¾ inch from the edge. Cut down to 1 inch from the base; don't cut all the way through. Scoop out the middle of the cake and discard.

Set the cake shell on a serving plate. Using a brush, moisten the bottom of the cake with the sugar syrup. Spread a layer of chantilly in the bottom and add the strawberries. Using a flat knife, spread chantilly around the sides and over the top edge of the cake. Put the remaining chantilly into a pastry bag and pipe rosettes around the rim. Refrigerate until ready to serve. This is best served on the day it is made.

genoise

4 extra-large eggs

⅔ cup sugar

1 cup all-purpose flour, sifted

filling

1–1¼ lbs. strawberries, sliced if large, cut in halves or quarters if small

freshly squeezed juice of ½ lemon

⅓ cup sugar

2 cups heavy cream, chilled

sugar syrup

3 tablespoons sugar

1 tablespoon brandy

a deep cake pan, 9 inches diameter, lined with parchment paper and buttered generously

a pastry bag with fluted tip

serves 8–10

Fresh berries are so tasty and good just as they are that it's tempting not to fuss with them too much. That said, they are also very good used in a crumble—the tastiest of baked desserts. If you wait for the right season, you can organize a family outing to go blackberry picking. Fruit gathered from the hedgerows will have the best flavor of all.

blackberry crumble

Preheat the oven to 350°F.

Put the blackberries in a bowl with the white sugar and the cornstarch and toss to mix. Tumble the berries into the buttered baking dish and set aside for 15–20 minutes.

Put the flour and butter in a large bowl and, using the tips of your fingers, rub the butter into the flour until the mixture resembles coarse bread crumbs. Stir in the brown sugar.

Sprinkle the mixture evenly over the berries and bake in the preheated oven for 45–50 minutes, until the top is golden brown.

Let the crumble cool slightly before serving with dollops of cream spooned on top.

12 oz. blackberries (about 2 baskets)

1 tablespoon sugar

1 teaspoon cornstarch

1 cup all-purpose flour

5 tablespoons unsalted butter, diced and chilled

¼ cup packed light brown sugar

heavy cream, to serve

a medium ovenproof dish, lightly buttered

serves 4

Apple pie must feature more often in people's memories of childhood than any other dessert. This one has a dark, spice-filled pastry that gives a delightfully different look and taste to a very old favorite.

dusky apple pie

Preheat the oven to 350°F and put a baking sheet in the oven to heat up.

Put the apple slices in a saucepan with the lemon juice, lemon peel, and sugar. Cover and cook over low heat for 15–20 minutes, turning the apples often so they soften and cook evenly. Set aside and let cool.

To make the pastry dough, put the flour, brown sugar, and spices in a food processor and process for a few seconds to combine. With the motor running, add the butter several cubes at a time. Add the egg and 1–2 tablespoons of cold water and process until combined. The dough will look dry and crumbly. Transfer to a bowl and knead to form a ball. Wrap the ball in plastic wrap and refrigerate for 30 minutes.

Cut the dough into two portions, with one slightly larger than the other. Roll the larger piece of dough between two sheets of waxed paper and use it to line the bottom and sides of the prepared tart pan. (Handle the dough with care—it will be quite crumbly.) Trim the edge of the dough to fit the pan.

Spoon the apples on top of the pastry base. Roll the remaining dough to a circle large enough to cover the base and place on top of the pie, trimming the edges to fit. Use a small sharp knife to make several slits in the dough. Put the pie on the hot baking sheet and bake in the preheated oven for 50–55 minutes, until the pastry is dark brown. Remove the pie from the oven and let it rest for 15–20 minutes before cutting into wedges and serving with vanilla ice cream.

8 tart green apples (such as Granny Smith), peeled, cored, and thinly sliced

2 teaspoons freshly squeezed lemon juice

2 thin slices of lemon peel

¼ cup sugar

pastry dough

2 cups self-rising flour

¾ cup packed light brown sugar

1 tablespoon ground cinnamon

1 tablespoon ground ginger

1 stick cold butter, cut into cubes

1 egg, lightly beaten

vanilla ice cream, to serve (optional)

*a loose-based fluted tart pan,
8 x 1½ inches high, lightly greased*

serves 8–10

Make these magnificent sweet creations to celebrate a special occasion or just to enjoy a sinful splurge. The combination of hot sauce, chilly ice cream, bananas, cherries, and crunchy nuts is irresistible.

banana splits with hot fudge sauce

To make the hot fudge sauce, put the chocolate, cream, and butter in a medium saucepan. When melted, add the light corn syrup, vanilla extract, and sugar, stirring constantly over medium heat. When nearly boiling, turn the heat down to low and simmer for 15 minutes without stirring. Let cool for 5 minutes before using.

To make the whipped cream, beat the heavy cream with the sugar and vanilla extract, and set aside.

Peel the bananas and cut them in half lengthwise. Take the dessert dishes and put 2 banana halves along the sides of each one. Put one scoop of each flavor of ice cream between the bananas. Top with one spoonful of the whipped cream, a sprinkling of pecans, and a cherry on top. Serve with a small pitcher of the hot fudge sauce to pour over the top.

4 small bananas

4 scoops each of strawberry, vanilla, and chocolate ice cream

½ cup shelled pecans, chopped and toasted

4 maraschino cherries

hot fudge sauce

3 oz. semisweet chocolate, chopped

¾ cup heavy cream

2 tablespoons butter

¼ cup light corn syrup

1 teaspoon pure vanilla extract

½ cup sugar

whipped cream

1 cup heavy cream

1 tablespoon sugar

1 teaspoon pure vanilla extract

4 banana split dishes

serves 4

A good cake for a party, this one looks wonderful and cuts easily.
The vanilla cake is baked in a square pan, cut into two strips, then
sandwiched with jam and topped with whipped cream and fresh berries.

raspberries-and-cream layer cake

Preheat the oven to 350°F.

To make the cake, put the butter in a large bowl,
then add the sugar, eggs, vanilla extract, milk,
flour, and baking powder. Beat with an electric
mixer or whisk using medium speed. When very
smooth and thoroughly mixed, spoon the mixture
into the prepared cake pan and spread evenly,
right into the corners.

Bake in the preheated oven for 25 minutes,
or until the cake just springs back when gently
pressed in the center. Remove the pan from the
oven and let cool for 10 minutes before turning
out onto a wire rack to cool completely.

With a large, sharp knife or bread knife, trim
off the edges, then cut the cake in half to make
2 strips.

Set 1 strip on a serving platter, then spread with
the raspberry jam. Top with the second layer of
cake and press down gently. Whip the cream
until very thick and soft peaks form, then spread
over the top of the cake. Decorate with the
raspberries and serve.

Store in an airtight container in the refrigerator
and eat within 3 days.

2 sticks unsalted butter, softened

1 cup plus 2 tablespoons sugar

4 extra-large eggs, at room temperature,
beaten

½ teaspoon pure vanilla extract

1 tablespoon milk

1¾ cups self-rising flour

½ teaspoon baking powder

filling and topping

5–6 tablespoons good-quality
raspberry jam

1 cup heavy cream, chilled

4 cups (1 lb.) small fresh raspberries

*a nonstick square cake pan,
9 x 9 x 2 inches, greased*

makes one 2-layer cake

Nearly every keen cook has a favorite carrot cake recipe. It's one of
those classics that can be made in an almost infinite variety of ways.
This version of carrot cake is crumbly and soft, and probably best eaten
with a spoon. If you are nervous about cutting the cake through the
center, simply spread the frosting over the top of the cooled cake instead.

carrot and walnut cake
with cream cheese frosting

Preheat the oven to 350°F.

Put the egg yolks and raw sugar in a large bowl
and beat for 2 minutes. Add the oil and baking
soda and beat until just combined. Fold in the
flour, baking powder, spices, carrot, and walnuts
until combined. The mixture should look quite
thick. In a separate grease-free bowl, beat the
egg whites with an electric whisk until they form
soft peaks, then fold them into the cake batter
in 2 batches. Spoon the cake batter into the
prepared cake pan and bake for 45–50 minutes,
until golden and slightly puffed on top. Let the
cake cool in the pan for about 10 minutes before
turning it out onto a wire rack.

To make the frosting, put the cream cheese and
butter in a bowl and let them come to room
temperature. Add the brown sugar and, using an
electric whisk, beat for 5 minutes, until there are
no lumps and the beaters leave a trail when
turned off. Add the maple syrup a little at a time
and beat for a further 2 minutes, until the
mixture is smooth and a spreadable consistency.
Carefully slice the cooled cake in half and spread
the frosting on the bottom layer.

2 eggs, separated

½ cup plus 1 tablespoon raw sugar

¾ cup plus 1 tablespoon light olive oil

1 teaspoon baking soda

¾ cup plus 2 tablespoons all-purpose
flour

2 teaspoons baking powder

1 teaspoon ground cinnamon

¼ teaspoon freshly grated nutmeg

1 cup grated carrot

⅓ cup walnut halves

cream cheese filling

8 oz. cream cheese

1 stick butter, diced

3 tablespoons brown sugar

2–3 tablespoons pure maple syrup

*a 7-inch diameter springform cake pan,
lightly greased*

serves 8

sauces
& preserves

This tangy sauce tastes nothing like the bottled variety you buy in supermarkets. It is traditionally served with meat, such as lamb or beef.

brown sauce

2 thick bacon slices, diced

2 tablespoons unsalted butter

2 shallots, finely chopped

1 carrot, finely chopped

1 cup mushrooms, finely chopped

2 tablespoons all-purpose flour

2½ cups beef stock (page 40)

1 bouquet garni (page 41)

2 tablespoons tomato concentrate

1 tablespoon dry sherry

sea salt and freshly ground black pepper

makes approximately 1¼ cups

Heat a saucepan and stir-fry the bacon for 3–4 minutes, or until brown and the fat has rendered into the pan. Add the butter and sauté the shallots, carrot, and mushrooms for 8–10 minutes, or until brown.

Stir the flour into the pan and cook for 2 minutes. Remove the pan from the heat and gradually stir in the beef stock until smooth. Return the pan to the heat and bring the sauce slowly to a boil, stirring constantly. Add the bouquet garni, tomato concentrate, and seasoning, partially cover the pan, and simmer very gently for 50–60 minutes, skimming the surface occasionally to remove the scum.

Strain the sauce through a fine strainer into a clean saucepan, add the sherry, and heat through. Serve hot or cool. To store, cover the surface of the hot sauce with plastic wrap, let cool, and refrigerate for up to 3 days.

Velouté, meaning "velvety" in French, is made with stock and enriched with egg yolks or cream. A chicken stock is used here—which makes it the perfect sauce to serve with chicken dishes—but you could also make velouté sauce based on other light stocks, such as fish.

velouté sauce

Put the stock in a saucepan and bring to a gentle simmer. Meanwhile, melt the butter in another saucepan and stir in the flour. Cook over low heat for 2–3 minutes, or until golden. Remove the pan from the heat and beat in the hot stock until combined.

Return the pan to the heat and bring to a boil, beating constantly until the sauce thickens. Simmer gently for at least 20 minutes, skimming the surface from time to time. When the sauce is glossy, stir in the cream and warm through without letting it come to a boil. Serve hot.

2 cups chicken stock (page 41)

2 tablespoons unsalted butter

2½ tablespoons all-purpose flour

3 tablespoons heavy cream

makes approximately 1¼ cups

Hollandaise is a smooth combination of butter, vinegar, and eggs. Rich and creamy, this sauce is pure heaven when accompanying such traditional partners as asparagus, artichokes, or poached salmon.

hollandaise sauce

Melt the butter very gently in a small saucepan. Pour it into a small pitcher through a cheesecloth-lined tea strainer to remove any excess milk solids.

Put the vinegar, shallot, salt, and 1 tablespoon water in a small saucepan and heat gently until the liquid is almost totally evaporated, leaving only about 1 tablespoon. Remove from the heat and strain into a glass bowl.

Place the bowl over a saucepan of gently simmering water (do not let the bowl touch the water). Add the egg yolks and, using a wire whisk, beat the mixture for 2 minutes, or until pale and frothy. Remove from the heat.

Using an electric whisk, beat in the melted butter, pouring it in in a slow, steady stream. Continue beating until the sauce becomes thick and velvety. Serve warm.

10 tablespoons unsalted butter

2 tablespoons white wine vinegar

1 shallot, finely chopped

a pinch of sea salt

2 egg yolks

makes approximately ¾ cup

variation: béarnaise sauce

Aromatic tarragon added to the basic hollandaise emulsion creates a classic sauce popularly served with pan-fried steak and french fries.

Follow the method above for hollandaise sauce, but replace the white wine vinegar with the tarragon vinegar and add the tarragon sprig while reducing. Stir the chopped tarragon into the finished sauce.

2 tablespoons tarragon vinegar

1 fresh tarragon sprig

1 tablespoon chopped fresh tarragon

makes approximately ¾ cup

A good barbecue sauce should be tangy, smoky, and rich—just like this one. It's wonderful with homemade burgers (page 82) but you can also serve it with barbecued beef, lamb, or chicken.

barbecue sauce

Put all the ingredients in a small saucepan, bring to a boil, and simmer gently for 10–15 minutes, or until reduced slightly, and thickened. Season to taste. Pour into a sterilized bottle (see note on page 169) and refrigerate for up to 2 weeks.

¾ cup tomato purée

⅓ cup pure maple syrup

3 tablespoons dark molasses

3 tablespoons tomato ketchup

3 tablespoons malt vinegar

3 tablespoons Worcestershire sauce

1 tablespoon Dijon mustard

1 teaspoon garlic powder

a pinch of smoked paprika

sea salt and freshly ground black pepper

makes approximately 1⅔ cups

The best gravy is made in the roasting pan while the cooked meat is left to rest. Gravy should complement the meat it is served with, not overpower it, and all you need is some pan juices, a little wine (white, red, or even Madeira or port), and some stock or water and you'll have a perfect, delicately flavored sauce to enhance your roast lunch.

gravy

Pour off and discard as much of the fat from the roasting pan as possible, leaving just the lovely meat juices. Put the pan over medium heat.

Add the wine and scrape the flavorsome, sticky bits from the base of the pan. Boil for 1–2 minutes, then add the stock and simmer for a further 3–4 minutes, or until slightly reduced. Strain before serving with the cooked meat.

cooked beef, chicken, pork, or lamb pan juices

½ cup white wine, red wine, or Madeira

⅔ cup chicken stock (page 41) or beef stock (page 40)

serves 4–6

Making mayonnaise calls for a little patience and a steady hand with the olive oil, but it is worth the effort. Use a mild, pure olive oil rather than extra virgin olive oil, which can be overly harsh and bitter.

mayonnaise

3 egg yolks

2 teaspoons white wine vinegar

1 teaspoon Dijon mustard

1¼ cups olive oil

sea salt and freshly ground white pepper

makes approximately 1¼ cups

Put the egg yolks, vinegar, mustard, and a little seasoning in a bowl. Using an electric whisk, beat until the mixture is frothy. Very gradually beat in the olive oil, a little at a time, mixing well after each addition until the sauce is thick and glossy and all the oil is incorporated. Cover the surface of the sauce with plastic wrap and refrigerate for up to 3 days.

note: If the mayonnaise is too thick, then slowly beat in 1–2 tablespoons boiling water to thin the sauce.

variation: aïoli

2–4 garlic cloves, crushed

Put the garlic in the bowl with the egg yolks, vinegar, mustard, and seasoning, and continue to follow the recipe as above.

A bowl of fresh tartare sauce enhances any type of fish or seafood.
This sauce is simplicity itself to make.

tartare sauce

Combine all the ingredients in a bowl and season
to taste.

½ quantity mayonnaise (page 158)

1 tablespoon finely chopped scallion

1 tablespoon capers in brine, drained and
chopped

1 tablespoon finely chopped gherkin

1 tablespoon chopped fresh flatleaf parsley

½ tablespoon chopped fresh dill

½ tablespoon snipped fresh chives

sea salt and freshly ground black pepper

serves 4

This is perfect for a lavish occasion. The rich tomato sauce infused with saffron provides a perfect base for fresh seafood, to serve with spaghetti or linguine. Saffron is not cheap, but you will need only a few threads—a very little goes a long way—and it's worth buying this aromatic spice for the flavor and rich color that it adds to food.

seafood sauce

Heat the olive oil in a large, wide saucepan and gently sauté the garlic and thyme for 3–4 minutes, or until soft but not brown. Add the tomatoes, stir well, then pour in the wine. Bring to a boil and simmer for 1 minute, then add the stock, saffron, and seasoning. Cover and simmer over low heat for 30 minutes.

Meanwhile, prepare the shellfish. Cut the lobster tails lengthwise down the center of the back and discard any intestinal tract, then cut, through the shell, into 4–5 pieces. (You can leave the shell on or take it off before cooking—if you leave it on, warn guests to watch out for the shell in the sauce.) Wash the mussels in several changes of cold water, scrub the shells clean, and pull out the straggly "beard" if still attached. Cut away the tough gray muscle at the side of each scallop.

Add the lobster and mussels to the tomato sauce and cook for 5 minutes, or until the mussels open. Discard any that remain closed. Add the shrimp and cook for a further 2 minutes, then add the scallops and cook for a further minute. Remove the pan from the heat and stir in the basil. Serve hot, drizzled with extra oil.

3 tablespoons extra virgin olive oil, plus extra to drizzle

2 garlic cloves, chopped

1 tablespoon chopped fresh thyme

1 lb. 6 oz. ripe tomatoes, peeled and finely chopped

$\frac{2}{3}$ cup dry white wine

$\frac{2}{3}$ cup fish stock (page 43)

a small pinch of saffron threads

2 x 12-oz. uncooked lobster tails

12 fresh mussels

12 large scallops

12 large uncooked tiger shrimp, shelled and deveined

2 tablespoons chopped fresh basil

sea salt and freshly ground black pepper

serves 4

The addition of chicken livers gives an extra dimension to this classic sauce. Bolognese is quick and easy to prepare but needs slow cooking to allow the flavors to develop. Serve poured over freshly cooked spaghetti or use as the base for lasagne or other baked pasta dishes.

bolognese sauce

Heat a saucepan and dry-fry the pancetta for 3–4 minutes, or until brown and the fat is rendered into the pan. Remove from the pan with a slotted spoon and set aside.

Add the olive oil to the same pan and gently sauté the onion, garlic, and thyme for 10 minutes, or until softened. Increase the heat, add the ground beef and livers, and stir-fry for 5 minutes, or until the meat is brown.

Add the wine and bring to a boil, then stir in the canned tomatoes, tomato concentrate, sugar, bay leaves, fried pancetta, and seasoning. Cover and simmer over low heat for 1–1½ hours, or until the sauce has thickened. Discard the bay leaves and season to taste.

4 oz. pancetta, diced

2 tablespoons extra virgin olive oil

1 large onion, finely chopped

2 garlic cloves, finely chopped

1 tablespoon chopped fresh thyme

1½ lbs. ground beef

2 oz. chicken livers, diced

1¼ cups red wine

2 x 14-oz. cans chopped tomatoes

2 tablespoons tomato concentrate

a pinch of sugar

2 fresh bay leaves (or 1 dried)

sea salt and freshly ground black pepper

serves 4–6

This thick, aromatic herb and nut sauce is used throughout the world to serve with pasta or grilled fish, or be stirred into vegetable soup. It needs no cooking, the ingredients are simply blended together for a wonderfully fresh taste. Once made, cover the surface with a little extra olive oil, seal in a container, and refrigerate for up to 3 days.

pesto

Put the basil, garlic, pine nuts, and salt in a mortar and pound to form a fairly smooth paste. Add the olive oil slowly until you reach a texture that is soft but not runny. Add the Parmesan and pepper to taste. Cover the surface with a little olive oil and refrigerate for up to 3 days.

tip: You can make this sauce in a food processor, but do not over-process otherwise the sauce will become too smooth.

2 handfuls of fresh basil leaves

1 garlic clove, crushed

2 tablespoons pine nuts

a pinch of sea salt

⅓–½ cup extra virgin olive oil

2 tablespoons freshly grated Parmesan cheese

freshly ground black pepper

makes approximately ⅔ cup

This is one of many variations on the original recipe for caesar salad dressing, first invented in the 1920s. Note that the ingredients include a raw egg yolk. If you prefer not to eat uncooked egg, you can follow an alternative recipe on page 21.

caesar dressing

Beat the egg yolk in a small bowl with the garlic, anchovies, lemon juice, Worcestershire sauce, and a little seasoning until frothy. Gradually beat in the olive oil a little at a time until thick and glossy. Add 2 tablespoons water to thin the sauce and stir in the Parmesan. Store in a screw-top jar in the refrigerator and use the same day. Shake well before using.

1 egg yolk

1 small garlic clove, crushed

2 anchovy fillets in oil, drained and chopped

1 tablespoon freshly squeezed lemon juice

1 teaspoon Worcestershire sauce

$\frac{2}{3}$ cup extra virgin olive oil

3 tablespoons Parmesan cheese, freshly grated

sea salt and freshly ground black pepper

serves 4–6

This is a classic salad dressing with the perfect balance of flavors—it is neither too sharp nor too oily. It keeps for several days in a screw-top jar in the refrigerator. Always shake well before using.

french dressing

Combine the vinegar, mustard, sugar, and seasoning in a bowl and stir until smooth. Gradually beat in the olive and safflower oils until amalgamated. Season to taste. Store in a screw-top jar in the refrigerator for up to 1 week. Shake well before use.

1 tablespoon white wine vinegar

1 teaspoon Dijon mustard

a pinch of sugar

$\frac{1}{4}$ cup extra virgin olive oil

2 tablespoons safflower oil

sea salt and freshly ground black pepper

serves 4–6

Crème anglaise—custard, by another name—should be stirred constantly over very gentle heat otherwise the egg yolks can curdle and spoil the texture. It is such a versatile sauce that it goes well with a variety of hot and cold desserts—most famously with apple pie.

crème anglaise

2½ cups milk

1 vanilla bean, split

6 egg yolks

2 tablespoons sugar

serves 8–10

Put the milk and vanilla bean in a saucepan and set over very gentle heat until it reaches boiling point. Remove from the heat immediately and set aside to infuse for 20 minutes, then discard the vanilla bean.

Beat the egg yolks and sugar together in a bowl until the mixture looks pale and creamy, then stir in the infused milk.

Return to the pan and cook, stirring constantly with a wooden spoon. Do not let the sauce boil.

When the mixture has thickened so that it coats the back of the spoon, remove from the heat. Serve hot, or if you prefer to serve it cold, cover the surface with plastic wrap to prevent a skin forming, and let cool.

Butter, sugar, and cream combine to make a wickedly rich toffee sauce, ideal for drizzling over ice cream, steamed puddings, and fruit.

butterscotch sauce

Melt the butter in a small saucepan. Add the sugar and corn syrup and cook gently until the sugar dissolves. Stir in the cream and vanilla extract and slowly bring to a boil. Remove from the heat and serve hot, or let cool and serve at room temperature.

3 tablespoons unsalted butter

¾ cup plus 2 tablespoons packed brown sugar

2 tablespoons light corn syrup

⅓ cup heavy cream

a few drops of pure vanilla extract

serves 6–8

Use a good-quality chocolate containing at least 70% cocoa solids to give a really rich, dark sauce—sublime with vanilla ice cream.

chocolate sauce

Combine the cream, chocolate, and butter in a bowl set over a saucepan of gently simmering water (do not let the bowl touch the water). Stir frequently until the chocolate has melted and the mixture is smooth. Remove from the heat, let cool for 10 minutes, then stir in the amaretto. Serve warm.

⅔ cup light cream

5 oz. semisweet chocolate, chopped

1 tablespoon unsalted butter

1 tablespoon amaretto, or another liqueur of your choice

serves 6–8

variation: white chocolate sauce

6½ oz. white chocolate, chopped

⅔ cup light cream

Combine the chocolate and cream in a bowl set over a saucepan of gently simmering water (do not let the bowl touch the water). Stir frequently until the chocolate has melted and the mixture is smooth. Remove from the heat, let cool for 10 minutes, and serve warm.

This is the sort of recipe that is kept alive by being passed down through generations of family cooks. The best thing is, like most chutneys, it is very simple to make. Serve in pork sandwiches, with all kinds of eggs, cheese, cold meats, or cooked breakfasts.

grandma's apple chutney

Chop the apples and onions very finely—this can be done in a food processor, but take care not to reduce it a pulp. It is important for the chutney to have texture.

Put the apples, onions, raisins, golden raisins, sugar, cayenne, mustard, ginger, salt, and the 2 cups malt vinegar in a large pan and simmer for 1–1½ hours over low to medium heat. Stir regularly to make sure the sugar does not burn, adding extra vinegar as necessary as the chutney reduces.

Turn off the heat and let the chutney settle. Stir and pack into the sterilized jars, leaving ½ inch headroom. Wipe the rims with a damp paper towel and cap the jars. Label when cooled.

Keep at least 1 month before you try it. This kind of chutney improves with age.

note: To sterilize jars, wash them in hot soapy water and rinse in boiling water. Place in a large pan and cover with hot water, then cover the pan with a lid. Bring the water to a boil and continue boiling for 15 minutes. Turn off the heat and leave the jars in the hot water until just before you fill them. Sterilize the lids by boiling for 5 minutes, or according to the manufacturer's instructions.

2 lbs. tart apples, such as Granny Smith, peeled and cored

1 lb. onions, quartered

⅔ cup raisins

⅔ cup golden raisins

2½ cups soft brown sugar

½ teaspoon cayenne pepper

½ teaspoon hot powdered mustard

½ teaspoon ground ginger

1½ tablespoons salt

2 cups malt or cider vinegar, plus 2 cups extra to add as the chutney boils down

3–5 pickle jars, 1 pint each, with screw bands and new lids, sterilized (see note)

makes 3–5 pints

Marmalade epitomizes leisurely weekend breakfasts in warm sunny kitchens. The beauty of this tangy marmalade, which uses three different fruits, is that it can be made in small quantities at any time of the year, not just when Seville oranges are in season.

chunky lemon, lime, and grapefruit marmalade

Scrub the fruit and pry out any stalk ends. Put in a pan and cover with 2 cups cold water. Set over low heat and cook until tender, 1½–2 hours.

Put the fruit on a chopping board to cool. Then cut in half, scrape out the flesh and seeds, and add to the pan. Bring to a boil and simmer for 5 minutes. Cut the zest into strips. Strain the water from the seeds and flesh and return the pulp to the pan, adding the zest and lemon juice. Discard the seeds and debris.

Add the sugar to the pan and bring slowly to simmering point, stirring until the sugar has dissolved. When the marmalade has become translucent, you will know the sugar has dissolved. Bring to a boil and boil rapidly until setting point is reached, 5–10 minutes.

Take the pan off the heat and test for set (see note). If the marmalade is not ready, return the pan to the heat to boil for a few more minutes and test again. When setting point has been reached, return to simmering point, then turn off the heat. Skim with a perforated skimmer, stir well, and let stand for 30 minutes. Stir and ladle into the sterilized jars, leaving ½ inch headroom. Wipe the rims with a damp paper towel and cap the jears. Let cool, label, and store in a cool, dark pantry.

note: To test for set, drop a teaspoon of marmalade onto a saucer that has been chilled in the refrigerator. Leave for 5 minutes. Push it with a finger—if it crinkles it is ready.

1 unwaxed lemon

1 small unwaxed pink grapefruit

1 unwaxed lime

freshly squeezed juice of ½ lemon

5 cups sugar

3 jam jars, ½ pint each, with screw bands and new lids, sterilized (see note, page 169)

makes about 1½ pints

Jam-making doesn't have to be as time consuming or complicated as many people think. This fruit-packed strawberry jam is quick and simple to make—and will fill your kitchen with a wonderful scent. Eat it with hot toast or scones and clotted cream (page 117).

strawberry jam

Wash the fruit and pat dry. Hull the strawberries and discard any that are damaged. Put in a large pan and cook gently over very low heat for a few minutes to start the juices running. Take care not to let the fruit burn. Let stand overnight. If you like, the fruit can be mashed at this stage.

Add the lemon juice and sugar to the fruit and bring to simmering point over low heat. Stir well while the sugar is dissolving. When the sugar has dissolved, increase the heat and boil rapidly for 10 minutes (remember to stir occasionally to make sure the pan does not burn), until the juice has reduced and the jam starts to thicken.

Take the pan off the heat and test for set (see note). If the jam is not ready, put the pan back on the heat to boil for a few minutes longer and test again. Repeat this process if necessary and remember to take the jam off the heat while testing, because over-boiling will ruin it.

When setting point has been reached, skim the jam with a perforated skimmer, stir it well, and let stand for 20 minutes for the fruit to settle. Stir and ladle into the sterilized jars, leaving ½ inch headroom. Wipe the rims of the jars with a damp paper towel and cap the jars. Let cool, label, and keep stored in a cool, dark pantry.

note: To test for set, drop a teaspoon of jam onto a saucer that has been chilled in the refrigerator. Leave for 5 minutes. Push it with a finger—if it crinkles it is ready.

2 lbs. small strawberries, picked in dry weather (8 cups)

freshly squeezed juice of 1 lemon

5 cups sugar

3–4 jam jars, ½ pint each, with screw bands and new lids, sterilized (see note, page 169)

makes about 1 quart

index

conversion chart

Volume equivalents:

American	Metric	Imperial
6 tbsp butter	85 g	3 oz.
7 tbsp butter	100 g	3½ oz.
1 stick butter	115 g	4 oz.
1 teaspoon	5 ml	
1 tablespoon	15 ml	
¼ cup	60 ml	2 fl.oz.
⅓ cup	75 ml	2½ fl.oz.
½ cup	125 ml	4 fl.oz.
⅔ cup	150 ml	5 fl.oz. (¼ pint)
¾ cup	175 ml	6 fl.oz.
1 cup	250 ml	8 fl.oz.

Oven temperatures:

180°C	(350°F)	Gas 4
190°C	(375°F)	Gas 5
200°C	(400°F)	Gas 6
220°C	(425°F)	Gas 8

Weight equivalents:		Measurements:	
Imperial	Metric	Inches	Cm
1 oz.	30 g	¼ inch	0.5 cm
2 oz.	55 g	½ inch	1 cm
3 oz.	85 g	¾ inch	1.5 cm
3½ oz.	100 g	1 inch	2.5 cm
4 oz.	115 g	2 inches	5 cm
5 oz.	140 g	3 inches	7 cm
6 oz.	175 g	4 inches	10 cm
8 oz. (½ lb.)	225 g	5 inches	12 cm
9 oz.	250 g	6 inches	15 cm
10 oz.	280 g	7 inches	18 cm
11½ oz.	325 g	8 inches	20 cm
12 oz.	350 g	9 inches	23 cm
13 oz.	375 g	10 inches	25 cm
14 oz.	400 g	11 inches	28 cm
15 oz.	425 g	12 inches	30 cm
16 oz. (1 lb.)	450 g		

recipe credits

Susannah Blake
Bird's Nest Cupcakes
Scones with Clotted Cream
    and Strawberry Jam

Maxine Clark
Barbecued Corn
Leek and Potato Soup
Mashed Potatoes
Parmesan and Butter Risotto
Pizza Margherita
Quiche Lorraine
Ricotta, Basil, and Cherry
    Tomato Cannelloni
Roasted Mediterranean
    Vegetables
Slow-roasted Tomatoes with
    Garlic and Oregano

Linda Collister
Breakfast Doughnuts
Chocolate Fudge Cookies
Cranberry and Bittersweet
    Chocolate Brownies
Mississippi Mud Pie
Raspberries-and-cream Layer
    Cake
Sticky Toffee Pudding

Ross Dobson
Blackberry Crumble
Carrot and Walnut Cake
Dusky Apple Pie

Sage Pork Chops
Scotch Broth
Smoky Sausage and Bean
    Casserole
Sticky Spareribs
Tarragon, Chicken, and Leek
    Pot Pie
Upside-down Heirloom
    Tomato Tart

Clare Ferguson
Cock-a-leekie

Tonia George
Beef Polpetti

Kate Habershon
Blueberry Sour Cream
    Pancakes

Jennifer Joyce
Banana Splits
A Bowl of Red
Chicken Noodle Soup
Manhattan Clam Chowder
New York Cheesecake

Jane Noraika
Garlic Mushrooms

Elsa Petersen-Schepelern
Caesar Salad
Cream of Mushroom Soup

Greek Salad
Minestrone
Mixed Green Salad
Salad Niçoise
Tomato Soup

Louise Pickford
Barbecue Sauce
Beef Stock
Best-ever Hamburgers
Bolognese Sauce
Bread and Butter Puddings
Brown Sauce
Butterscotch Sauce
Caesar Dressing
Chicken Stock
Chocolate Sauce
Crème Anglaise
Fish Stock
French Dressing
Gravy
Hollandaise Sauce
Mayonnaise
Pesto
Seafood Sauce
Tartare Sauce
Vegetable Stock
Velouté Sauce

Anne Sheasby
Old English Trifle

Sonia Stevenson
Creole Gumbo
Traditional Fish Pie
Yorkshire Puddings and
    Horseradish Sauce

Fran Warde
Beef and Carrot Casserole
    with Cheesy Dumplings
Meat Loaf with Two Sauces
Roast Chicken with Lemon,
    Thyme, and Potato
    Stuffing
Roast Potatoes
Sausage and Bacon Toad-in-
    the-hole

Laura Washburn
Chocolate Mousse
Beef and Potato Gratin
Crème Caramel
French Onion Soup
Macaroni Gratin
Ratatouille
Steak and Fries
Strawberry Shortcake
Wilted Greens

Lindy Wildsmith
Chunky Lemon, Lime, and
    Grapefruit Marmalade
Grandma's Apple Chutney
Strawberry Jam

photography credits

Key: a=above, b=below,
r=right, l=left, c=center.

Caroline Arber
Pages 2, 5br, 9, 30, 60, 90,
92, 95

Martin Brigdale
Pages 1, 5ar, 7, 12, 32, 50,
57, 58, 63, 64, 71, 72 80,
84, 86, 99, 103, 115, 116,
119, 128, 131, 132, 136,
139, 144

Peter Cassidy
Pages 5al, 11, 14, 16, 19,
20, 23, 28, 31, 45, 46, 53,
76, 124

Tara Fisher
Pages 168, 171, 172

Richard Jung
Pages 54, 67, 79, 89, 100,
104, 108, 110, 120, 140,
143, 148

William Lingwood
Pages 27, 68, 96, 112, 135

Diana Miller
Pages 123, 147

David Munns
Page 24

Noel Murphy
Pages 35, 36, 49, 107

William Reavell
Page 75

Yuki Sugiura
Pages 8, 38

Debi Treloar
Pages 4, 5bl, 13 inset

Ian Wallace
Pages 40, 42, 83, 150,
152–166

Polly Wreford
Pages 13 main, 127